A RETURN TO GRANDPA'S HOUSE

Stories of an American Family

MICHELE L. LARSON

iUniverse, Inc.
New York Lincoln Shanghai

A RETURN TO GRANDPA'S HOUSE
Stories of an American Family

iUniverse books may be ordered through booksellers or by contacting:

iUniverse
2021 Pine Lake Road, Suite 100
Lincoln, NE 68512
www.iuniverse.com
1-800-Authors (1-800-288-4677)

Because of the dynamic nature of the Internet, any Web addresses or links contained in this book may have changed since publication and may no longer be valid.

The views expressed in this work are solely those of the author and do not necessarily reflect the views of the publisher, and the publisher hereby disclaims any responsibility for them.

ISBN: 978-0-595-43946-1 (pbk)
ISBN: 978-0-595-68492-2 (cloth)
ISBN: 978-0-595-88267-0 (ebk)

Printed in the United States of America

This book is for my nieces, nephew, sisters, cousins, and their children. It is also for my parents, aunts, and uncles. May we may always know, remember, and cherish the legacy of love and family which we have been given.

Contents

Acknowledgments

I express many thanks to my sister Christine for her encouragement and hours of editorial help and suggestions. Thanks also to my mom for her proofreading assistance, and to my dad for bringing me into this branch of my family tree.

Introduction

It was the wind in the trees that made her realize this was really home. She stood in the yard under the trees, and she remembered how she had stood here and listened to the wind when she was a child. She was older now, and the trees were taller, but the wind was still the same. After all this time, it had called her back, called her home, and she had listened. She had come back home.

It was funny, really. Most people talk about home and are referring to the house where they grew up. But she had not grown up here, not in that respect. Her father had. It was his parents' house, Grandpa and Grandma's place. But, like her sisters and cousins, she had spent countless hours here on the farm. In their own way, they all thought of it as home. For years, it was the gathering place for picnics and holidays, reunions and parties. Just as Grandpa and Grandma were the foundation of the family, this house was its soul. Grandpa and Grandma had been gone for many years now. They rested in the cemetery a few miles down the gravel road; but a part of them was still here. You could feel it when you walked in the house. You could almost smell Grandma's cinnamon rolls or sugar cookies or dough-nuts. You might think you saw Grandpa's sermon notes on the dining-room table next to his Bible. You could almost hear their voices as you looked out the window toward the barn. Yes, a part of them was still there; she had no doubt of that.

For a couple of decades, it had been a winding journey that took her to places far from the small town where she had grown up. But, gradually, the road had circled back. More and more often, she found herself stopping to listen for the wind in the cottonwood trees. One day when she heard it, she decided it was time to go back and see if things really were as she remembered them or merely nostalgic wishes that had somehow been distorted by time and distance. Now, standing here under the trees, she knew the answer. This was no distortion. The memories were accurate and as real to her as the day they took place. She looked up into the branches of the old cottonwood tree near the edge of the field. It stood taller than any other tree on the farm. She still remembered the summer day when she was a little girl and walked with Grandma out to that tree and asked her why it had a white stripe all the way down its trunk.

"Because," Grandma said, "it's been struck by lightning. Every year, that tree is struck by lightning, sometimes more than once."

"But, Grandma, doesn't that hurt the tree?"

"Well, I suppose it might, but never bad enough that the tree will die. That tree must be almost one hundred years old by now and doesn't seem to be bothered by a little lightning."

She never forgot that conversation. With each passing year, as the tree continued to stand straight and true with that white lightning stripe down its trunk, it became a symbol. For her, that cottonwood tree began to represent endurance and healing and renewal, because nothing bad could last as long as that cottonwood tree stood alive and well and strong. She walked over to the old tree and touched the scarred white trunk. Hearing the wind in the tall, high branches, Marlena whispered words of her own. "Grandpa and Grandma," she said, "I'm home."

Chapter One
An Old House in the Country

"Buying an old house in the country" is what her sister had called it. Why would you? Why would anybody? It's nothing but wood and glass and dirt. At least, that's what most people thought. Really? She wasn't even going to live there? Well, why not? Then why in the world was she buying that place, if she wasn't even going to live there? It just didn't make sense. City people—she was one, you know, one of those city people. She may have grown up here, but she moved on long ago; so what was this all about anyway? What was she doing? What was she thinking? Why was she buying it? What's wrong with her? Really, what's the point?

The point, indeed. The point was that this was about her family, her history, her family's history. It was about a place that was very nearly lost to strangers who didn't know the stories, wouldn't cherish the memories, and wouldn't yearn to go back to the place that had formed, shaped, and nurtured all of them. The point, indeed, was that this wasn't just a house. It wasn't just a building and a piece of land. This was who she was, who they all were. This was about remembering who they were and where they came from. It was about sharing the hopes, the history, and the very place with the next generation. It was about connecting those children with a past they could be proud of. It was about grounding them for their future. It was about providing them with roots that ran so deep they would be unshaken, regardless of what life handed them in the years to come.

An old house in the country? No. No, the farm site in southwestern Minnesota was far more than that; indeed it was. It was all about the memories they had—she, her sisters, and her cousins. And as time went on, it was also about the children in the next generation and the new memories, the ones they would make as they shared the stories and the memories of their past.

Chapter Two
Butchering Chickens

As we get older and recall special memories, they are often of holidays or family celebrations. But, sometimes, those memories may be of different type of events. The memory may be wrapped around what could otherwise be considered a rather gruesome occasion. Such was the case of butchering chickens, when all the grandchildren and their mothers gathered at Grandpa and Grandma's house.

"Grandma! Where's Meredith?"

It was the first thing she asked when she got to Grandpa and Grandma's house that early morning. The old house was already filled with noise; children's laughter and shouting, adults' hurried conversations, pots and pans clattering in the kitchen. It was early on a summer morning, and there had already been many hours of frantic activity. This was one of the children's favorite days, and one of the adults' busiest. Today was the day the chickens were butchered, and everyone, even the youngest child, had a job to do.

Grandma was in the kitchen boiling water in huge pans that were only used at this time of the year. Aunt Cheryl and Mom were taking things from the kitchen outside to the butchering table: knives, pans, and buckets. The feathers would be placed in boxes, crates, or pails. The children were collecting those and bringing them over to the butchering table. Even the cats and dogs sensed that this was a special day and ran around excitedly.

Grandpa had gotten up very early, caught the chickens, and put them in cages. Every year, Grandpa seemed to ignore the bloody marks on the backs of his hands, where the chickens had pecked him as they tried to get away. All the chickens were in crates now, and all the crates were stacked up in the back of the old pickup truck, which was parked near the butchering area. Grandpa was the only one who actually killed the chickens. It was always that way. He had a special way of taking care of things, and everyone respected how it was done.

The butchering was done outside, near the machine-shed shop. There was a tree near there that had a branch about five or six feet off the ground. Grandpa always hung about seven pieces of black twine from that branch. Each piece of twine was about twelve inches long and had a little loop knotted at the end of it. The twine strings swayed in the wind like seven little black nooses. Near the branch, Grandpa had his old scalding pail. It looked like an old milk pail, about two feet tall. The butchering table was two sawhorses with some old planks laid over them. Years of butchering were evident in the dark-brown spots that stained the boards.

When everything was just about ready, Grandpa reached into the first cage and started pulling out the chickens. Oh, the chickens fought and squawked, but they were no match for Grandpa! In no time, he had their feet tied-up in the little black twine nooses, and when he let them go, they were hanging upside down. When the chickens were hung in all the twine nooses, Grandpa got his knife. It was time for the unpleasant, but necessary, part of this work. Grandpa always used the same small, shiny stainless-steel paring knife. He grabbed each chicken by the neck and forced open its beak. Then Grandpa's normally arthritic hands made one swift, smooth motion and cleanly slit the chicken's throat. Grandpa went down the line, doing the same thing to each chicken.

Within minutes, the chickens were dead, their eyes glassy, their lifeless bodies twisting and turning at the end of the twine, blood dripping from their beaks out onto the ground. This was what the cats and dogs were waiting for! Licking the blood off the ground was a special treat they enjoyed. No matter how much the children tried to shoo them away, they kept coming back for more.

Grandpa let the chickens hang for a few minutes, and then he sent one of the children into the house to tell Grandma they were ready for the boiling water. Everyone told the children to step away as Grandma poured the water into Grandpa's scalding pail. All six children, Mom, and Aunt

Cheryl took their seats on stools or upside-down pails around the butchering table. Grandpa took the first chicken down from the string, held it by its feet, and pushed it head-first into the scalding pail. He always had his stick nearby and used it as a plunger to push the chicken up and down deep into the pail. After a few immersions, he pulled the chicken out of the scalding pail and threw it onto the butchering table, where steam rolled off the hot, wet feathers. Then Grandpa took down the next chicken and did the same thing, until all the chickens had been scalded.

Mom and Aunt Cheryl made sure that all the children got a chicken to work on; then they and Grandpa would get the last three. If you started right away, when the chicken was hot, the plucking was easy. You could take great handfuls of feathers out at one time and have the chicken bare in just a few minutes. The wings were the hardest, and the pinfeathers. Everyone hated pinfeathers. They never came out easy and had to be plucked out one at a time. Sometimes it was funny to see that some of the chickens had hair on their skin under all those feathers. Everyone was supposed to work very fast to get as many feathers out as they could before the chickens cooled off. The children's hands were covered in feathers as they tossed the feathers into the crates and pails under the tables. Sometimes they missed, and feathers were all over the ground around the butchering table. The cats and dogs liked feathers too—not as much as the blood, but all day long, you could see the cats and dogs running around with feathers around their mouths.

When everyone was nearly done with his or her chicken, Grandpa grabbed the next seven chickens and hung them from the twine and started the process all over again. Grandma would come out from the farmhouse with more boiling water and collect the plucked chickens, place them in pans, and take them into the house. In-between times, she began fixing a big dinner for everyone; usually meatballs, potatoes, vegetables, and sometimes, if she had time, fresh cinnamon rolls! The cycle continued all morning, several times, until all the chickens had been butchered.

By then, it was time for dinner. Everyone washed up really well to get all the feathers and chicken blood off their hands. Then they sat down at the big kitchen table to eat. Grandpa always prayed and thanked God for the bountiful day and the many blessings he had bestowed upon them, the food he had given them this day, and the family gathered there. Then they ate. Butchering chickens had made everyone very hungry! The children hurried through dinner so they could go outside. Their part of butchering was done, and they had all afternoon to play. Usually, the boys got to go out and play first, while the girls helped Grandma with the dishes.

Grandpa, Mom, and Aunt Cheryl still had more work to do. They had to go down in the basement and cut up all the chickens—"cleaning them," Mom called it. Sometimes the children wanted to help with that part, too, but the adults always said no. That part was too dangerous for little children, with all the big knives around. So the children were content to run and play in the barn, see the cows, visit the pigs, and walk in the woods. Many times, the girls would go out on the open porch and play dress-up. Grandma had an old trunk there. She had filled it with discarded dresses and aprons, and it was always fun to try on different outfits. The porch also had an old bed that the children pretended was a trampoline. They would have great fun jumping on it, but they always had to be careful of the big living-room window. They didn't want to lose their balance and bounce through the window!

Throughout the afternoon, the children would wander down to the basement and see what the adults were doing. The cold, wet, fleshy smell got stronger the farther down the basement stairs they went. There were pans of icy, cold water with chicken parts in them. The chicken innards were in big pails underneath the table Grandpa and Mom were working on. Aunt Cheryl would come down with fresh pans of ice water and then take the other pans, with the chicken in them, back upstairs. Grandma and Aunt Cheryl worked at the kitchen sink, packing the chickens into plastic bags that went into clean half-gallon milk cartons.

In the middle of the afternoon, Grandma always told everyone to come in for lunch. The adults had coffee, but Grandma always made green or orange Kool-Aid with a can of orange-juice concentrate in it for the children. She also made bread, butter, and jam sandwiches with her home-made strawberry jam; and she had doughnuts and sugar cookies.

Grandma's sugar cookies were always perfect—big and thick and sugary—and never burned.

After lunch, Grandpa and Mom went back downstairs to finish cutting up the chickens. It was always close to suppertime before they got done. Aunt Cheryl and the cousins usually ate supper with Grandpa and Grandma, stayed overnight, and went home the next day. Sometimes, Dad would come out to the farm after work, and they would all have supper together with Grandpa and Grandma. Grandma said Mom had worked so hard that day, she didn't need to go home to fix a meal for everyone; she would feed them there.

After supper, Grandpa had evening devotions. He read aloud from the Bible or a prayer book. Then he talked about what he had read. He always ended by saying a prayer and thanking God for the family gathered around the table and the day they had spent together. There were offers to help with the dishes before going home. But Grandma said they had done enough; there were enough people there to get the dishes done. So, instead, everyone helped Mom and Dad pack up the freshly butchered chickens and take them out to the car.

It was often getting dark by the time they drove home. The purple shades of twilight stretched over the horizon as far as the eye could see. When the car windows were open, the mosquitoes might have flown in. The children could hear their buzz before they felt their bite and tried to swat at them before they landed. The children could also hear the songs of the grasshoppers and other night-bugs, as the sun began to set over the northern plains. It had been a long, busy, happy day. The children's eyes might have begun to close during the short ride home, but they fought to keep them open, because they didn't want the day to end. Mom was tired, too. When they got home, she had to put all the chickens in the freezer. Then she had to give the children baths and make sure they got all the feathers, dirt, and chicken blood off their arms and legs before they went to bed. The children never fought about going to bed on chicken-butchering day. Butchering chickens always made them tired.

As they drifted off to sleep that night, the children thought back to their responsibilities as little helpers. But what they did not realize was how important those roles would be in their futures. For that day, they did more than just help put meat away for the winter. They were also stockpiling memories for the years ahead and would carefully guard those reserves of their summer days spent in the country.

Chapter Three
Christmas

Summertime was not the only time the children and grandchildren gathered at Grandpa and Grandma's house. There were certain times of the year when it was tradition to have everyone come back home. No matter where you were or what you were doing, you always made an effort to find your way back to the big old house in the country for these occasions. One of those times was during the cold, dark December days of winter, a time that everyone looked forward to: Christmas.

Yes, it was Christmas. Well, it was almost Christmas; actually, it was the Sunday before Christmas, and the day of the big family Christmas party at Grandpa and Grandma's house. The cousins, aunts, uncles, great-aunts, and great-uncle would all be there, and the grandchildren were very excited. They loved Christmas and getting presents, but they also loved seeing their cousins and playing with them. Of course, they had to go to church and Sunday school first; but right after that, they went home, loaded up the car with food and presents, and drove the few miles to Grandpa and Grandma's house. It was a cold, sunny December day. Huddled in the backseat, the grandchildren looked out the frosty windows at the empty, snow-covered fields and barren, leafless trees.

Lots of cars were already at Grandpa and Grandma's house. Grandpa had church services there, and people came early for that, but Mom always said they needed to go to their Sunday school instead. Grandpa had usually finished with church by the time they got there. But sometimes, when they walked in the house, if it was very quiet, they knew that church was still going on. Then they would wait quietly in the kitchen, the only sound being that of food cooking in pots on the stove, until Grandpa said the final prayer and church was done.

Wonderful smells always greeted everyone when they arrived at Grandpa and Grandma's house. The most distinctive aromas were the wood smoke from the old wood-burning stove, turkey roasting in the oven, and coffee brewing in the coffeepot. The cousins were always happy to see each other and would run off to play until dinnertime. They would run up and down the stairs or play with some toys, laughing and talking with each other. Mom, Grandma, and the aunts stayed in the kitchen getting the dinner ready. The great-aunts, Grandpa's sisters, offered to help but were usually content to sit in the living room with the men.

Dinner was always held in two rooms. The adults ate in the dining room, and the children ate in the kitchen. The women filled two dishes of everything, one for each room. When everyone was seated, Grandpa asked Uncle Thomas to start the table blessing, and everyone joined in, singing to the "Old Hundredth" tune:

> "Be present at our table, Lord!
> Be here and everywhere adored.
> These mercies bless and grant that we
> May feast in Paradise with Thee.
> Ah-men."

Then Grandpa prayed (sometimes, Mom said, until the food was cold). After Grandpa's prayer, everyone would dig into the scrumptious meal: turkey, mashed potatoes and gravy, vegetables, salad, bread, and the children's favorite—lefse, rolled up with butter and sugar! Grandma usually had a dog, and sometimes a cat, in the house. They stayed in the kitchen, eagerly waiting for the scraps of food the children would inevitably drop on the floor. Somehow, there was always enough food for everyone to eat and still have much left over. It was a little like the story in the Bible about feeding the five thousand with five loaves and two fishes.

After dinner, while the men went back to the living room to talk about things related to farming, like the weather and the price of corn, the women would do the dishes. Usually, Grandma and Aunt Rose put away the food, Mom washed, the great-aunts dried, and Aunt Cheryl put away the dishes. Sometimes they tried to get the children to help, but usually they were too excited to be very helpful. It always took quite awhile to get all the dishes done.

One of the chores the children always did enjoy wasn't a chore to them at all, it was fun: putting more wood in the old cookstove in the kitchen. Everyone wanted to put something in the fire. The small children weren't able to both hold up the lid and put the sticks in all at the same time, so the older children held the lid up so the little ones could drop the wood into the stove.

The children's voices and laughter got progressively louder as their excitement mounted. They knew that as soon as the women were done in the kitchen and went in the living room, that the best part of the day had arrived: presents!

The front porch was filled with presents, and sometimes the back porch had presents too. Sometimes, there were so many presents in the house that a few people had left their gifts in the car. The children always got to pass out the presents. Some of the smaller children couldn't read, so they had to go ask their moms whose names were on the gift tags. Grandpa always sat in his favorite chair, and you could see the happy, contented expression on his face as he watched his grandchildren flit among the adults with the brightly-wrapped packages. The children worked fast, and it didn't take long to pass out all those presents. One of the adults would finally ask, "Is that everything?" The children would all shout, "Yes!" and then there was the happy, chaotic sound of tearing paper, gleeful shouts, and pleased "thank you's."

The great-aunts had never had children of their own, but they loved to buy presents for all the little ones. Nearly every year, the presents they gave were soft and squishy, and the children often knew what was in them before they opened them—fabric. Mom and Aunt Cheryl both liked to sew, and the great-aunts always gave the children fabric that their moms could make into pretty dresses or handsome shirts. In later years, the great-aunts discovered mail-order catalogs, and Aunt Cheryl said they spent many happy hours poring over the catalog pages looking for just the right gifts for everyone.

After all the presents had been opened and everyone had checked to see what everyone else had received, Grandpa liked to have them sing Christmas carols. Meredith, because she was the oldest grandchild and had been taking piano lessons, was often asked to play the carols on Grandma's old upright piano. Everyone joined in the familiar carols: "Away in a Manger," "Joy to the World," and Grandma's favorite, "I Heard the Bells on Christmas Day." Although everyone sang, Uncle Thomas had the best singing voice, and he could always be clearly heard above everyone else.

The winter afternoons were short, and though the sun shone brightly through the windows, outside there were long, dark shadows across the clean, white snow as the winter sun crept closer to the frozen horizon. Despite the cold outside, the sound of songs and crackling wood fire lent special warmth to the house and the people inside as they shared the celebration of the Savior's birth and the joy of each other's company.

After the singing, Grandma declared it was time for the afternoon lunch. No one, of course, was ever hungry, since they had all eaten so much for dinner. But it was never even a consideration that you wouldn't have lunch; that was just the way things were. The turkey was retrieved from the refrigerator (or the unheated back porch, if the refrigerator had been too full) and served cold with bread and butter. The lefse, salad, and pies were placed on the table in the kitchen. Grandma made a fresh pot of coffee, and Mom and the aunts got out the special Christmas sweets that were served only at lunch: krumkake, rosettes, homemade fudge and candy, and always, Mom's fancy cookies that she made only at Christmastime and put on pretty glass plates.

For lunch, everyone went to the kitchen for their food. After loading up their plates, they found seats in the dining room or living room where they could eat, drink their coffee, and reminisce about the day and Christmases past. The children were usually more subdued, having grown tired from all the Christmas activities. Meredith and Marlena often went and sat among all the coats on Grandma's bed. There, they shared their "girl secrets," away from their little sisters and brothers.

As the day drew to a close, people began to gather up their presents, dishes, and children. The moms packed things into boxes and bags, and the dads took them out to the cars and somehow found a way to fit every-thing into the trunks. Then they started the cold cars and turned on the heaters to warm up the cars before their families came outside. Grandma helped the moms find coats and missing scarves and mittens. Then she, Grandpa, and Uncle Thomas would stand on the front porch and wave good-bye and wish "Merry Christmas" to everyone as they bundled up and went out the door into the dark night. It had been another wonderful Christmas together as a family. Everyone said a silent prayer of thanks for the day and for each other as they made their way home under the bright, twinkling stars of a clear, cold winter night.

Chapter Four
Fourth of July

Holidays were special times at Grandpa and Grandma's. Christmas was certainly everyone's favorite holiday, but there were also other memorable holiday times. Grandpa was particularly fond of the summer gatherings, which were so different from the inside festivities of the winter celebrations. Grandpa loved picnics. Whenever possible, he tried to have the entire family gather for a Fourth of July picnic. He delighted in the preparation, and a few days before the picnic, he always bought the biggest watermelon he could find and lots of Crush pop in several flavors. There was the usual Orange Crush, but Grandpa also found Grape Crush and Strawberry Crush. He bought several wooden cases of the bottled pop, each case being a different flavor.

The cousins, aunts, uncles, great-aunts and great-uncle all came for the picnic. Grandpa and Grandma had a picnic table in the front yard, and Grandma scrubbed the table clean before putting her vinyl tablecloth on it and securing the corners so that it would not blow off in the summer breeze.

Mom and Aunt Cheryl would bring salads. One of them always brought a gelatin salad with shredded carrots and pineapple in it. Most of the children didn't like that one; vegetables, especially carrots, in gelatin just didn't seem right. But they liked Grandma's potato salad and the other good things Grandma had for the picnic.

In later years, when Mom and Dad brought their charcoal grill, there would be hamburgers and hot dogs. Before that time, only hot dogs were cooked for the picnic. In fact, it was an official "wiener roast." Grandpa would gather all the grandchildren around him and tell them very seriously that they all had to go into the woods with him to look for the "wiener-roasting sticks." Then Grandpa would grab his walking-stick and head toward the trees. Although Grandpa had a cane, he always seemed to prefer a stout branch from one of the trees. He had used the stick so often that it had been worn smooth by time and use.

One-by-one, the grandchildren trailed after Grandpa, looking for just the right sticks to cook the hot dogs. The ideal sticks were twenty-four to thirty inches long and had branches with three or four forks on the end of them. Each time the children thought they had found a good stick, they asked Grandpa, "Is this a good stick, Grandpa? Will this one work for roasting wieners?"

"Sure, sure," Grandpa often said, and they continued on this special treasure hunt.

When all the wiener-roasting sticks had been gathered, Grandpa and the grandchildren walked back to the picnic table. Then Grandpa took out his knife and started whittling the ends of the branches into sharp, speared points. One-by-one, the grandchildren handed him their branches so he could turn them into genuine wienie-roasters!

After that, it was time to build the fire. This was usually done on the driveway, because it was dirt and there was no danger of sparks spreading. When the fire was good and hot, Grandma brought out the hot dogs. Grandpa had all the grandchildren line up with their wiener-roasting sticks, and he put a hot dog on each pointy end of the stick. Then the children walked over to the fire and roasted the wieners. Sometimes, the adults had to help them turn their sticks so the hot dogs didn't get burned on one side. Occasionally, they were too late, and a few hot dogs got very black with charcoal.

Grandma, Mom, and the aunts brought out the paper plates and napkins, the hot dog buns, condiments, salads, potato chips, and other food. When the hot dogs were done, the children went to Grandpa. He traded the roasted hot dogs for uncooked ones and sent the children back to the fire. The children always enjoyed this day, because *they* got to do all the cooking for everyone—even the adults—so they thought they were pretty important!

When all the hot dogs had been roasted, everyone sat down at the picnic table and bowed their heads to sing the table-blessing before eating. The food was, of course, delicious. Often, the adults said these were the best hot dogs they had ever eaten, and the children beamed with pride.

When everyone had eaten their fill, Grandma went inside to get the watermelon. Grandpa often helped her cut it, and soon everyone had a large, red, juicy slice of watermelon. It was customary to spit the seeds on the ground, and the children often decided to have a contest to see who could spit seeds the farthest.

Still, the picnic wasn't over. After everyone had eaten watermelon, Grandma went back into the house for her bag of large, puffy marshmallows. Grandpa told all the children to go get their wienie roasting sticks and come over to him. Then he put one marshmallow, sometimes two, on each prong of the stick, and the children went over to the fire to roast marshmallows. These cooked much faster than the hot dogs, and sometimes, if the children weren't paying attention, the marshmallows even caught fire! Then they yelled for their moms or dads to come help them and put out the fire.

Roasted marshmallows tasted best if they were eaten right away, when they were black and crispy on the outside and hot and gooey on the inside; but you had to be very careful that you didn't burn your mouth. It was best to eat the marshmallows in one bite, but if you couldn't, the insides of the marshmallow often stretched into a long, sugary string when you bit into it.

Finally, when everyone had eaten until they couldn't eat anymore, the picnic dinner ended. The women cleared the table and took food inside. They enjoyed the picnics because there were very few dishes to do. The men often continued to sit at the picnic table and visit, while the children ran off to play on the farm. There were always new calves to visit. When the children tried to pet the calves, their hands were tickled as the calves licked at their fingers. There were kittens to look for in the hayloft, or baby pigs to hold. Or sometimes, the grandchildren would have a silo-climbing contest. They usually didn't get very far up the silos before one of the moms noticed and yelled at them to get down.

Time seemed to slow down on those hot afternoons. The air was filled with the sounds of summer: birds chirping, cicadas and grasshoppers singing, flies buzzing, adults talking, and children laughing. Gradually, the shadows lengthened as the sun slipped westward. The children began to tire, and the adults gathered their belongings for the return home. Everyone agreed—it had been another wonderful summer day, another happy Fourth of July.

Chapter Five
Picking Potatoes

There were many good times with Grandpa and Grandma that did not center on a holiday. Sometimes, in fact, the focus of a family get-together was to help Grandpa with his work. Grandpa was a farmer. But more than that, he was a gardener; and his favorite crop was potatoes. He loved planting them, he liked picking them, he enjoyed peeling them, and always, he took pleasure in eating them. He took a special delight in his grandchildren when they, too, liked to eat lots of potatoes.

Grandpa was very particular about when the potatoes got planted. He was a religious, pious man who looked to God and the Bible for all the guiding principles of his life. But when it came to planting potatoes, he also went by the moon and the calendar. Somehow, there was a formula about the moon's cycle in relation to Easter that would determine the appropriate time for planting potatoes. Once Grandpa decided when this would be, everyone helped: Mom, Dad, and the grandchildren.

The children were given ice-cream pails filled with seed potatoes (wedges of potatoes with the appropriate number of eyes), and they would walk down their rows and place the potatoes a few inches apart from each other. If their pails emptied, Grandpa was always ready to fill them up again. Every year, Grandpa insisted that they plant three kinds of potatoes: red ones, white ones, and russets. Grandpa and Grandma said russet potatoes were the best potatoes for making lefse, and they always wanted to be sure there were plenty of good russet potatoes for that.

Like everything else in the garden and fields, the potatoes grew all summer long. In early summer, the first potatoes, though small, would be ready to eat. It was common to see Grandpa wearing his old straw hat, sitting at the picnic table peeling large pans of potatoes he had brought in from the garden. This was a ritual he enjoyed all through the summer; although, occasionally, if it was too hot outside, you would find him sitting on a stool in the kitchen with his pan of potatoes. Grandma was thankful for this, since she didn't really like to peel potatoes.

Sometime in October, Grandpa would decide it was time to harvest the potatoes. Everyone always hoped for a warm, sunny Saturday afternoon, but often the sky filled with dark grey-blue clouds as the wind blew blustery promises of winter. Grandpa, Uncle Thomas, or sometimes Dad, would plow up the potatoes so that they lay on top of the soil. Then Grandpa hooked up his little trailer to the small John Deere lawn tractor and drove down to the potato patch. Mom, Dad, and the grandchildren followed him with several empty pails. Then everyone took a pail and walked down a row collecting potatoes.

The children always enjoyed picking potatoes, because it was the one time they were allowed to play in the dirt. Their hands got dirty, their shoes got dirty, and sometimes, their pants got dirty if they lost their balance in the loose soil and fell down. The children also enjoyed picking potatoes, because they could turn it into a contest about who had the largest, smallest, ugliest, or strangest potato.

As their pails filled, everyone walked back to the lawn tractor and dumped their pails into the little trailer. When the trailer was empty, the potatoes made very loud "thunk, thunk, thunk" noises as they hit the bottom of the trailer. The sound of potatoes being poured into the trailer grew muffled as the trailer filled.

Pail after pail, row after row, the potatoes were picked. Grandpa always made the children feel important and exclaimed what good workers they were as they came with their pails full of potatoes. He promised that there would be "plenty of potatoes" to last through the winter.

Mid-afternoon, Grandma would come out and tell everyone to come in for lunch. Mom took the children into the bathroom and tried to scrub all the dirt off of their hands so they could eat. Often, she used the rough Lava soap, which the children didn't like. The adults drank coffee, but Grandma had hot chocolate for the children, to "warm them up," she would say. Grandma had bread, butter, and jam sandwiches to eat, and plenty of her homemade doughnuts.

After lunch, everyone went back to the potato patch to finish picking the potatoes. They always got done before the sun went down, but the children's fingers had usually gotten cold by the time they finished. The little trailer was now filled with potatoes, and Dad put a board across the back end of the trailer so the potatoes wouldn't fall out. Then came the best part—riding with Grandpa on the little lawn tractor as they pulled the potatoes up to the house! One of the children sat in Grandpa's lap, and one sat on the fender next to him. Or sometimes, if there was room, the children might get to ride in the trailer with the potatoes. Grandpa started up the little tractor, drove out of the potato patch, up the ditch, onto the driveway, and back to the house. Mom and Dad walked behind, picking up any stray potatoes that fell out of the trailer.

At the house, the children ran inside to wash their hands and talk with Grandma or play the piano. Their work was done. Grandpa backed the trailer up to the basement window of the house. Dad went downstairs and took out the window. Then, with Dad working in the basement and Grandpa and Mom working outside, the potatoes were placed in pails, passed through the window, and dumped into the root cellar, where they would stay for the winter. When all the potatoes were safely inside the root cellar, Mom, Dad, and Grandpa went in the house to visit. It had been a long, busy day; but, as Grandma said, "many hands make light work."

During those days, it wasn't just potatoes that were being cultivated; it was also a good work ethic. The children were learning that you never quit until the job was done—something they later recalled as they were preparing for exams in high school and college. The children were learning that goals were achieved when everyone worked together, a lesson they later demonstrated in their work lives. The children were learning that it was OK to get their hands dirty, and if you went home tired at the end of the day, it meant you put in a hard day of honest work, and that was something to be proud of. Yes, it had been another good potato harvest; but it had also been another successful lesson in honing the children's work habits and preparing them for their futures.

Chapter Six
The Seventh Grandchild

With time and tradition comes predictability. But every now and then, maybe after several years of the same routine, life has a way of shaking things up with a surprise. With the surprise comes a new routine and new traditions, each filled with their own joy; and pretty soon, it's hard to imagine that life was any other way. So it was when Mom was going to have a baby. After six years, there would be another baby in the house. The two sisters would soon have a baby brother or baby sister.

When Mom and Dad told Grandpa and Grandma the news, the girls remember Grandpa smiling contentedly and looking proud. Then he told them something none of them had ever known; he had always wanted seven grandchildren. This new baby would be number seven. From the time he was very young, he said he wanted four children and seven grandchildren because he had been born on April seventh—the seventh day of the fourth month. Seven was a special number for another reason, since biblically, it was a complete number. Because Grandpa was a pastor, such biblical symbolism was important to him. He and Grandma had four children, two boys and two girls. For six years, there had been six grandchildren. Now, there would be seven; Grandpa's wish would be fulfilled. The man born in the fourth month on the seventh day would have four children and seven grandchildren. The number, and the cycle, would now be complete.

Grace, the youngest grandchild, was born in September 1973. From the beginning, as the seventh grandchild, she had a special relationship with Grandpa. His oldest grandchildren were almost in high school and busy with many activities, so it brought Grandpa much joy to have a little one around again.

Grace, too, enjoyed the time she spent with her grandpa. Her sisters were older and not always around when she and Mom went out to the garden. So, even if there wasn't anyone else to play with, she got to spend time alone with Grandpa. They walked down to the barn and saw the dairy cows. Some were quite congenial and let their noses be petted. They visited the steers and fed them some of the tall grass that grew near the garden and the steer yard. They went to the hog barn and watched and listened to the pigs as they grunted and chased each other out in the hog yard. They stopped at the next building and looked at the chickens ("laying hens," Grandma called them). The hens were always a little intimidating with their squawking and wing-flapping, so Grace and Grandpa often stood outside and looked at the chickens through the wire mesh screen door of the hen house, rather than going inside.

Or sometimes, she and Grandpa might just walk together, enjoying each other's company, like they did one special fall day. It was a beautiful sunny day, warm enough for short sleeves without a jacket. The leaves were just starting to turn colors, and there was a slight autumn breeze. Grandpa was wearing his old straw hat, and had his walking-stick in one hand. In the other hand, he clasped the small hand of his seventh grandchild. Together, the old man and the little girl with long hair the color of corn silk walked under the trees with falling yellow leaves swirling around them. It was the autumn of one life intersecting with the spring of another life. The man at the beginning of the cycle, and the little girl who had completed it, making a memory that would last a lifetime.

Chapter Seven
Grandpa and the Baby Chicks

There's no magic formula for making special memories, but if there was, it would certainly include children and baby animals, especially baby chicks. There is a certain innocence and trust and sense of wonder when children and young animals interact. The grandchildren were fortunate that they grew up with those experiences. Every spring, there were new chicks on Grandpa and Grandma's farm. Grandpa always bought his chicks already hatched. He never hatched them on the farm. Each spring, when the chicks arrived, Grandpa called Mom and Dad and asked them to bring the grandchildren out to the farm to see the baby chicks. When they went to the farm, usually on a weekend, Grandpa would come out to meet them. He would wear his cap and worn jacket, find his walking-stick, and lead the procession out to the brooder house. The brooder house was a place just for baby chicks, and it was placed in the grove of trees, away from the chickens and other animals.

When they got to the brooder house, Grandpa opened the door, and the air was filled with the sound of fifty cheeping baby chicks. A large incubator took up most of the space inside the brooder house. The incubator, which kept the chicks warm, was a metal, somewhat circular, structure. The outside edges of it had little flaps that would raise up, revealing small troughs for chicken feed. The metal flaps were constantly rattling and banging as the chicks ate and ran around. The floor of the house was filled with wood shavings, providing the chicks with a soft, absorbent surface.

Grandpa would reach down and catch one of the baby chicks and hold it. The grandchildren lightly touched its soft feathers, as it wiggled and squirmed in Grandpa's hands. Then he would hand the chick to one of the grandchildren to hold. Of course, the other grandchildren then wanted to hold their own chick, so Grandpa caught a chick for each of them. The chicks gently scratched at the children's hands with their tiny yellow-orange feet. They might also peck at the children's hands with their little beaks, but they were so small, it never hurt. It felt more like a pencil-point tapping at them than a bite.

As the grandchildren got older, they wanted to catch the chicks themselves. It was never as easy for them as it was for Grandpa. The chicks were tiny, but they were very fast and could turn corners quite sharply. The grandchildren also had to be careful they didn't squeeze or crush the chicks when they caught or held them. The chicks were so small; it was like holding tiny little yellow balls of cheeping fluff. The grandchildren loved to hold the chicks up to their cheeks and feel the soft, downy feathers against their skin and listen to their little peeps. As they got more proficient, the grandchildren would set their chicks down and try to catch other ones. Eventually, the chicks realized what was happening, and they would all run under the incubator and congregate near the center, where they were out of reach of little hands. The grandchildren might wait a few minutes to see if the chicks would come back out. Usually, they didn't. All the exercise they had gotten running away from little children had made them tired!

Then everyone would leave the brooder house. Grandpa shut the door behind them. He made sure the door was tightly latched to protect the baby chicks from cold and other things, like foxes, that liked to eat baby chicks. Then they all walked up to the house, leaving the baby chicks warm and snug in their little house in the woods.

Each year, the children were older, but they still looked forward to the arrival of the baby chicks every spring. In holding the little yellow balls of feathers, they began to realize that they held not only their memories of other springs and other baby chicks; they also held their futures. Just as the chicks would grow and mature, the children realized that they, too, were growing up, and each spring, they came a little closer to leaving home and reaching for their dreams. Somehow, it seemed that Grandpa knew that too. He wasn't just raising chickens on the farm; he was also shepherding his grandchildren on the road to adulthood.

Chapter Eight
Taking Grandpa Lunch

Rural life has different patterns and rhythms than the urban experience. Certainly, the pace is different. The population is usually different. The choices, whether it's shopping or entertainment, are different. Sometimes, even the language or names of the meals are different.

There were always five meals on the farm: a big country breakfast, morning lunch, dinner (which is what the noon meal was called), afternoon lunch, and supper (which is what the evening meal was called). Lunch, especially afternoon lunch, was a favorite time. By that time, the better part of another day was finished. Afternoon lunch meant there were only another few hours of work before looking forward to a little evening relaxation, and finally, a good night's sleep.

When the children were out to visit, especially in the summer, they looked forward to the afternoon lunch. Sometimes Grandpa and Uncle Thomas would take their lunch into the fields with them. Or, they might come back to the house for lunch. Other times, Grandma and the children would take lunch out to them in the field.

Grandma's lunches usually consisted of bread, butter, and jam sandwiches, made with her homemade strawberry jam. There were also some of Grandma's homemade doughnuts, or some of her sugar cookies, or maybe, as a special treat, some of her homemade cinnamon rolls. If Grandpa and Uncle Thomas weren't coming back to the house, Grandma, Mom, and the children would eat lunch together. Grandma always made her special Kool-Aid for the grandchildren. It was usually orange or green Kool-Aid, but she always mixed in a can of orange-juice concentrate to give it more flavor.

When they were through with lunch, Grandma made fresh coffee and put it in a thermos. She then packed sandwiches, doughnuts, and cookies into the old, black, metal lunch pail that she would take to Grandpa and Uncle Thomas. Sometimes, she had an extra thermos of the Kool-Aid that she packed, too. If the children were within earshot, she would call for them and ask if they wanted to come with her. Since it sounded like a great adventure, the children always said yes.

Grandma went out to the step with the lunch pail and found her walking-stick. Then she and the children set off on their journey with Grandma's little brown dog, Mitzi, trotting beside them. They walked past the machine shed, through the woods, past the big, new, steel machine shed, to the edge of the field. They could hear Grandpa and Uncle Thomas's tractors in the distance, so they knew they wouldn't have to wait very long. On those hot summer afternoons, they enjoyed standing under the trees, listening to the birds and crickets as the wind rustled the leaves of the corn.

Soon, Grandpa and Uncle Thomas came down the field towards them. After working hard all afternoon, Grandpa and Uncle Thomas were ready for a short break. They were always happy to see Grandma, and, Grandpa especially, enjoyed it when the grandchildren came with her out to the field. If they had a hayrack, Grandpa and Uncle Thomas usually sat on the back of it while they ate their lunch. The children and the dog would run and laugh and play games, being careful not to stray too far from Grandpa, Grandma, and Uncle Thomas. They had been warned about little children getting lost in the fields, and they knew that it was dangerous. When they grew tired of playing, they crawled up on the hayrack to rest and sit beside Grandpa and Uncle Thomas and visit with them while they ate their lunch. Sometimes, Uncle Thomas had coffee, or sometimes he preferred the Kool-Aid Grandma had brought. But no matter how hot it was, Grandpa always had his afternoon coffee.

All too soon, lunch was over, and Grandpa and Uncle Thomas announced that they had to get back to work. The children helped pack up the wrappers and napkins and jumped off the hayrack into the field. They said good-bye to Grandpa and Uncle Thomas. They knew that they would be leaving for home long before Grandpa and Uncle Thomas finished their work in the fields. Then they, Grandma, and the little brown dog started walking back to the farmhouse as the sounds of the tractors faded away into the distance.

Little did the children know that, at some point, they would experience days where "dinner" was a fancy restaurant meal in the evening and "lunch" was a quick meal around noon before an afternoon meeting. In that context, "lunch," as they had shared it with Grandpa, Grandma, Uncle Thomas, and the little brown dog, no longer existed. Only if they closed their eyes and thought back to those summer treks to the field could they remember what Grandma's doughnuts tasted like. And maybe, just maybe, if they listened really hard, they still might hear the sounds of tractors in the distance.

Chapter Nine
The Preacher's Room

During our lifetimes, we come in contact with all kinds of people. Some become lifelong friends; others are present for only a short period of time, but leave an indelible mark. The grandchildren met a variety of people on Grandpa and Grandma's farm, especially during the summer. Grandpa was a pastor. He was the only pastor for the remaining North American churches of a small Norwegian Lutheran synod. The synod's membership had been dwindling for years, and Grandpa was basically a circuit pastor, visiting small congregations in South Dakota, Wisconsin, and Minnesota every few weeks. When those congregations were still active, it was common for Grandpa and Grandma to have people visit them regarding church business, especially during the summer, when the annual conferences were held. The small congregations also supported missionaries, and sometimes, even the missionaries came to visit Grandpa and Grandma. Whenever there were important church guests, they stayed in a special room—The Preacher's Room.

The Preacher's Room was at the top of the stairs and was the largest and nicest of the five upstairs bedrooms. It was a corner room and had two windows, one facing south and one facing west, so it was always bright and sunny. Over the years, there were many guests that stayed in The Preacher's Room. One summer, there were some very special visitors that stayed for several weeks. They were a Norwegian missionary family serving in Japan but visiting in the U.S.

The family consisted of the pastor, his wife, and their three young children; two little girls and a little boy. The oldest girl, Ingrid, was five, the younger girl was three, and the boy, who had just started walking, was about two. The grandchildren were eager to meet the missionary children and hear their exciting stories about living in distant lands and faraway countries.

The two younger Norwegian children were quite small and didn't really understand English, so they didn't play with the other children very much. But Ingrid and the grandchildren became great friends. Since she had lived most of her life in Japan, she thought the farm was fascinating and loved to see the animals and hear the grandchildren tell stories about them. They spent hours walking through the barns, looking for kittens and playing hide-and-seek. Ingrid, at the age of five, spoke three languages: Norwegian, Japanese, and English. Once, one of the grandchildren asked her if someone asked her something in one language, would she be able to think about it and answer them in another language? She said yes and didn't seem to understand why that sounded strange and difficult.

One day, when the grandchildren came out to visit, there was a great commotion in the house. Apparently, the little Norwegian boy had thrown one of his toys in the downstairs toilet and then flushed it. Needless to say, that caused some plumbing problems. Grandpa, Uncle Thomas, and the Norwegian pastor had just fixed it. Grandma had been in the bathroom mopping up, and the little boy was crying because he had just been punished. Mom sent the grandchildren outside, where they would be out of the way. Ingrid, not wanting to be in the middle of everything, decided to go outside with them. The girls went down to the cattle barn, away from little brothers, broken toilets, and wet floors.

Later, when they walked back up to the house, Ingrid's mother came outside and asked her, in English, where she was. She explained that she had just gone down to the barn to get out of everyone's way. Then Ingrid's mom started talking to her in Norwegian. Ingrid started answering her in English, and then, in mid-sentence, switched to Norwegian. The grandchildren could no longer understand what was being said, but they could tell from the tone that Ingrid was being scolded. Later, when her mother went into the house, the grandchildren asked Ingrid what her mom had said.

"Oh," she said, "my mom didn't like it that I disappeared without telling her. She wanted me to watch my little sister while she cleaned up my little brother, and when she couldn't find me, she got upset."

"Why did your mom start talking to you in Norwegian after she was talking to you in English?"

"She just wanted to. She likes talking Norwegian better."

"Was it because she didn't want us to hear?"

"Yes, I think so."

"Well, we're used to that. Our Grandpa and Grandma sometimes switch from speaking English to talking Norwegian when we're around. We know it's because they don't want us to hear what they're saying; that they're probably talking about something they don't want us to know. So, can you still play, or do you have to go inside?"

"Well, I should go in and help my mom," she replied; and she did.

The grandchildren saw Ingrid and her family one more time after that day. They knew it would be the last time they would ever see each other, and they were a little sad. But they were also thankful for the fun times they'd had. What they had expected to be another routine summer had turned out to be something quite special with the missionaries' visit.

Finally, it was time to say good-bye. The grandchildren went home knowing that the next time they went to visit Grandpa and Grandma, Ingrid and her family would be gone. The house would be quieter than it had been the last few weeks. Things would be like they were before. Grandma would have stripped the beds and washed the sheets and cleaned the house. There would be other days with other visitors, although never any quite like these visitors. But, always, The Preacher's Room was there, ready to shelter and provide rest to the various travelers that passed through Grandpa and Grandma's lives.

Chapter Ten
The Fortieth Anniversary

There are many milestones that mark the passage of time in family life: births, deaths, birthdays, and anniversaries. Although each occasion is important, some are more memorable than others are. Often, it is the passage of time that causes some of those occasions to acquire elevated importance. This can be due to the event itself. Or, in retrospect, it may be the realization that the event in some way marked the beginning of a different journey. Such was the case with Grandpa and Grandma's fortieth anniversary.

The excitement had been building for several weeks. Mom had been baking lots of special, fancy cookies. She had been poring through her cookbooks, looking for new recipes. She had talked with Aunt Cheryl, who was also doing a lot of baking, and they were making sure that each of them was baking different kinds of things. The grandchildren had been assigned jobs. Invitations had been sent. Flowers had been ordered, and notices had been placed in the local newspapers. Grandpa and Grandma were celebrating their fortieth wedding anniversary, and there was going to be a party.

The anniversary celebration was, of course, going to be at Grandpa and Grandma's house. They wouldn't think of being away from home for such a special occasion. It was agreed that the open house would be in the summertime, when the weather was warm and it was easy for everyone to travel. Aunt Rose had been home on occasional weekends to help Grandma clean the house. Grandpa loved having company, and he was already looking forward to seeing special visitors. Several of the pastors he knew, as well as other important church people, were expected.

The grandchildren were excited, too. Meredith, because she was the oldest and least likely to burn herself, would be pouring coffee. Marlena was excited that she'd be serving punch. One of the boys would be stationed at the guest book, while another was responsible for keeping track of any presents people might bring.

Finally, the special Sunday arrived. Fittingly, it was beautiful, warm, and sunny. After church, Mom, Dad, and the girls went home and got ready for the big day. They ate a quick dinner before the girls changed into the long dresses that Mom had made for them. It was, after all, a very special occasion. Then they loaded up the car with all the cookies Mom had made and drove out to the farm.

Aunt Cheryl and Uncle Nathan and all the cousins, as well as Aunt Rose and the great-aunts and great-uncle, were already there. They were just finishing up the dinner dishes. Mom and Dad started bringing in all the cookies. Soon, Mom, Aunt Cheryl, and Aunt Rose were busy with all of the preparations: setting up tables, covering them with tablecloths, getting out the punch bowl and flowers, preparing the cookie plates, laying out dishes and napkins, setting out the cake, making the coffee, and, finally, pinning a boutonniere on Grandpa's lapel and a corsage on Grandma's dress. Then Aunt Cheryl came downstairs. Her hair was all done up in back, and she was wearing an old-fashioned dark dress.

"Why, it's Grandma's wedding dress!" someone exclaimed.

The children didn't believe it at first. That couldn't be Grandma's wedding dress; it wasn't white! How could you have a wedding dress that wasn't white? But it was Grandma's dress, they were told. Back then, it wasn't unusual for women to wear dark dresses at their weddings.

The first guests arrived nearly half an hour early. Thankfully, everything was ready. The grandchildren eagerly invited the guests to sign the guest book and asked them if they wanted punch or coffee. Grandpa and Grandma were sitting in the dining room, and they and their guests were soon visiting away. Before long, more people arrived. Then more people came. One of the aunts told Grandpa and Grandma they should move to the living room. Since it was a bigger room, it would be easier for people to visit with them.

Soon, the house was filled with people. Mom, Aunt Rose, Aunt Cheryl, and some of the other women were extremely busy filling the cookie plates and keeping paper plates and napkins on the table. Mom had been asked to bring some of her pickles, and everyone liked them, so she was constantly refilling the pickle dishes. Meredith announced that she was almost out of coffee, and Aunt Rose went to start another pot. Marlena said she needed more punch, and another woman came to fill up the punch bowl. The boys were running out of room to place the presents, and the basket for cards was nearly full. Once, when she walked to the kitchen, Marlena looked out the dining room window and saw that the driveway and yard near the machine shed were filled with cars. In fact, there were so many cars that some of them were parked near the garage, back by the trees.

The grandchildren had been excited about this day for a long time, but they soon realized, with so many people, that this was what the grown-ups called "work." Several times, one of the aunts remarked that they were glad the children were there to help, or they wouldn't be able to keep up with everything!

Eventually, everyone got a chance to visit with Grandpa and Grandma. But there were so many guests that Grandpa and Grandma never had a chance to leave their chairs in the living room. Grandma finally sent one of the grandchildren to the kitchen for a glass of water. Then Aunt Rose realized that Grandpa and Grandma hadn't eaten yet. She fixed each of them a plate of food and carried it to the living room, where Grandpa and Grandma could continue to visit between bites of food.

Finally, toward late afternoon, new guests stopped arriving. Gradually, the crowds in the house and on the lawn thinned out. The grandsons had already abandoned the gift and guest book duties. Meredith didn't want to pour any more coffee, and Marlena was tired of serving punch. They, too, decided they wanted to fix a plate and eat, and they took their food out to the living room, just like the grown-ups had. Mom said they should sit at the table so they didn't spill anything, but one of the aunts told her that there had already been so much food dropped on the floor in there, a little more wouldn't matter. All of Mom's cookies were delicious. Every single new recipe she had tried had been a success. The cake was moist, the frosting was rich and creamy, and the fancy homemade mints, in the shapes of leaves and flowers, were very tasty.

Soon, someone said something about cleaning up and putting things away. Grandma said, "Uff da, what a bunch of people." Grandpa just smiled and chuckled softly. Then someone said, "Pictures! We never took any pictures!" The grandchildren were again rounded up, the cameras came out, and the flashbulbs started going off. When the picture-taking was done, Mom and the aunts wearily began clearing the tables and packing up the food. Thankfully, they hadn't run out of food, because Mom and Aunt Cheryl had both planned for an army of people; but they were still surprised at how little was left.

Soon, everything was put away. Aunt Rose said she would stay and help Grandma vacuum and clean the following day. The children that were left in the house were sent out to round up their brothers and sisters. They all came back in to wish Grandpa and Grandma a happy anniversary before leaving for home.

Forty years was a lifetime, in some respects. In forty years, Grandpa and Grandma had gone from a young married couple to parents, property owners, and grandparents. Their family had grown from two to fifteen in two generations. Forty years of joys and sorrows, struggles and triumphs. Forty years of friends and family. In one afternoon, they had celebrated it all, in the house that Grandpa and Grandma called home.

Chapter Eleven
Grandpa Cleaning Eggs

There were always certain images that came to mind when one thought of Grandpa: Grandpa with his straw hat and his walking-stick; Grandpa driving his little riding mower around the farm; and Grandpa picking and cleaning eggs. Picking eggs was a daily chore on the farm. Each day, Grandpa would go out to the hen house with his yellow-wire egg basket and pick eggs. Sometimes the grandchildren wanted to accompany him, even though some of the hens frightened them. A few of the hens had bald patches where they used to have feathers, because the other, younger hens would pick on them. Grandpa would reach under the chickens to get the eggs, and sometimes the hens would peck the back of his hand. If his hand started to bleed, the grandchildren asked him if he was hurt. He always said no, and continued collecting eggs. Most of the time, Grandpa's chickens laid eggs that were white; but occasionally, there were hens that laid brown eggs. Sometimes, when Grandpa picked the eggs, there would be little streaks of blood on them. This, too, concerned the grandchildren, and they asked Grandpa if it hurt the chickens to lay eggs.

"Oh, no," he answered, "sometimes those things just happen."

When the eggs had been gathered, Grandpa took them up to the house and down to the basement. At the bottom of the stairs and to the left was an old yellow pantry cabinet. This was where Grandpa kept his eggs after they were cleaned. There were usually one or two baskets of eggs sitting on the floor next to Grandpa's stool. Grandpa would sit on his stool in front of an old table and wipe each egg to clean off any dirt or blood. If he found any cracked eggs, he would set those aside for Grandma to use. Cracked eggs couldn't be sold. The good eggs would then be placed in open, molded, fiber egg-trays. These looked like the bottoms of egg cartons, but much larger and without the sides or lids. Each tray held more than one dozen eggs, and the trays could be stacked in such a way that the eggs didn't break when another tray was set on top of it. The filled egg trays were then kept in the old yellow cabinet before being packed into heavy cardboard boxes.

Often, if the grandchildren came out to visit on a winter evening and they didn't see Grandpa right away, they would ask where he was. Grandma would usually reply that he was downstairs cleaning eggs. The grandchildren would go down to the basement to see Grandpa and watch him. Sometimes, they asked if they could help, but Grandpa usually said, no. He knew that their little hands might unintentionally break some of the eggs. If the grandchildren persisted with their offers of help, he might say, "No, because if you break the eggs, then Grandpa would have to spank." After that comment, the grandchildren went upstairs fairly quickly, figuring they should find something a little less hazardous to help with.

Grandpa and Grandma had enough "laying hens," as Grandma called them, to supply themselves and some of their children's families with eggs and then sell what was left. Periodically, the egg truck would stop at the farm to pick up the eggs that Grandpa and Grandma had for sale. The grandchildren were always excited if they saw the egg truck slow down and start turning into the driveway. They would run to find Grandma and announce, "The egg truck is here! The egg truck is here!"

When the truck pulled up to the house, Grandma met the driver at the door. She and the driver then went down to the basement, and the driver collected the full cases of eggs and took them upstairs and out to his truck. The grandchildren were always amazed at how many eggs the truck could hold.

"That's an awful lot of chickens to lay all those eggs," they would say.

After he was done loading up the eggs, the truck driver told Grandma that she and Grandpa always had some of the nicest eggs he ever saw. Then he had Grandma sign something, so the egg company could pay them for their eggs.

After the truck drove away, the grandchildren went downstairs to see if there were any eggs left in the basement. Usually there were a few. The driver left any cases that were only partially full of eggs. These would be filled and picked up on the next visit.

So, the sequence of events would begin again. The chickens would lay more eggs, Grandpa would sit on his stool in the basement and clean them, and the old yellow cabinet would again be refilled with trays of eggs waiting to be packed into cases. Picking eggs was just another small part in the bigger cycle of things on the farm. Even though things appeared to have a beginning and an end, they also seemed to continue indefinitely. It was a little like the sun coming up over the silos each morning, always introducing another day—a new day with new surprises and different challenges. As the grandchildren moved toward adulthood, they became more aware of these rhythms and patterns. They realized there were constants in life they could count on: Grandpa, chickens, eggs, and sunrises.

Chapter Twelve
The Old Schoolhouse

There is a sense of history with country life. Often, it is family history. With each visit to Grandpa and Grandma's house, some history was imparted, and some was created. But there is also other history. One of the best examples was visible from Grandpa and Grandma's farm: the old one-room schoolhouse. The old schoolhouse was a tan, stucco, sturdy-looking structure, and it sat on a corner where two gravel roads intersected. The grandchildren had always taken the schoolhouse's existence for granted. It was just another landmark on the way to Grandpa and Grandma's house. For, when you turned east at the schoolhouse, you turned onto the road that ran past Grandpa and Grandma's house. Theirs was the first house on the left after the schoolhouse.

It had been many years since children learned there, but the grandchildren loved to hear stories about how their dad would walk to the schoolhouse each day when he was a boy. He was the oldest and went all the way through eighth grade at the schoolhouse before transferring to the high school in town. When they were old enough, his brother and sisters also walked to the one-room schoolhouse. All of the children in grades one through eight had the same teacher, because that's the way things were done in one-room schoolhouses. Because their dad was the oldest, it meant he had extra responsibilities. He tried to look after his brother and sisters when they were at school, for instance. He also didn't always get to study as much as the others if Grandpa needed help with chores.

The one-room schoolhouse was closed before the youngest girl, Rose, completed all eight grades. Times were changing, and progress beckoned in a new world that looked at many things, including one-room schoolhouses, as quaint and old-fashioned. In a modern world, it was far more efficient to bus the country children to larger schools in town. Grandma said she remembered when they closed the school. They auctioned off many of the schoolhouse supplies: desks and chairs, books, pictures, and even some of the blackboards.

Many one-room schoolhouses fell into a state of disrepair when they were no longer used. Many others were torn down. Once landmarks of education and testimonies of the pioneer spirit, they simply disappeared from the landscape as if they, and an entire way of life, had never existed. It was not so with this schoolhouse. Oh, sure, in the summer, the grass around the schoolhouse would often grow tall and unmanageable. But then a neighbor would come with his hay mower and mow it down so it lay in great piles, just like the hay in the field. The schoolhouse itself was always maintained and kept up, because, in fact, it was still used. It wasn't used for school, of course, but for township meetings or 4-H club or voting on election day. This was the building where the people had chosen to gather. So, as they had for generations, the people would make their way to the schoolhouse to conduct their business, celebrate their good news, and support each other during hard times. For, though the way of education had changed, the important things about life in the country had not. Those things stood the test of time, just like the old schoolhouse.

Chapter Thirteen
Summer Evenings

Summer is every child's favorite season of the year. There is no school to get up for and no homework to do, so there is no reason to go to bed early. There are just long, lazy, sunny days spent running, playing, and exploring. Summer evenings are particularly pleasant times. The grandchildren often spent summer evenings on the farm with Grandpa and Grandma. If Mom and Dad needed to work in the garden, the children were left to play by themselves. But often, they would interrupt their play to help Grandpa or Grandma, because sometimes helping Grandpa and Grandma was even more fun than playing.

Grandpa and Grandma always had two kinds of chickens: the "laying hens," as Grandma called them, and the chickens that were raised for butchering. The laying hens were confined to the hen house and ventured outside only as far as the concrete slab connected to the hen house. This was fenced in so the hens would not wander off. The other chickens spent their lives in the brooder house in the woods. When they were baby chicks, they were kept safely inside the brooder house, but as they matured, they were allowed outside during the day to wander among the trees, pecking for bugs and worms and other food.

Each evening, before it got dark, the chickens had to be gathered back into the brooder house. The grandchildren always volunteered to help with this. It was fun looking for the chickens and chasing them through the trees, trying to get them back in their house. Some of them were very sneaky, zigzagging through the woods, trying to elude the grandchildren. Grandpa and Grandma were always thankful for the grandchildren's help, because they could just watch while the children did all the running.

It usually didn't take long to get the chickens back into the brooder house. After the first couple chickens went in, the others always seemed to know what was expected of them and quickly followed. The grandchildren then walked in wide circles out from the brooder house, making sure there were no renegade chickens trying to avoid capture. The grandchildren knew that if a chicken was left in the woods overnight, it would probably not survive. Either a fox or raccoon would be sure to make a tasty meal of it.

After the chickens were tucked in for the night, and if it wasn't too windy, Grandma gathered the garbage that needed burning. Grandma had a burning barrel, where she burned nearly all of their garbage. The burning barrel was away from the house, near the road that went out to the field. It was an old fifty-five gallon drum that Grandma had used for years, so it had a black and rusty appearance. Grandma had the paper and other burnable garbage in a paper grocery bag, and she put the whole bag into the burning barrel. Then she lit a match on the inside of the barrel. The grandchildren were always amazed that Grandma could light a match like that without a matchbook.

Grandma stood vigil, with her little brown dog, Mitzi, at her side, while the garbage burned. She said it was important that the sparks and cinders not get away and start a fire somewhere. The grandchildren knew that helping Grandma watch the fire was an important job. They always told Grandma about any ashes that they saw that looked like they might escape from the burning barrel. When the garbage had nearly burned out, Grandma took her walking-stick and poked at the ashes in the barrel. She wanted to make sure the embers were dying and the fire wouldn't flare up when she walked away.

After burning the garbage, Grandma usually took laundry off the clotheslines. The grandchildren had a little red wagon they played with, but Grandpa and Grandma had also begun to use the wagon as a handy little cart. Grandma would go back to the house for her empty laundry baskets, place them in the little red wagon, and take the wagon out to the clotheslines to get the clothes. Like all American women, Grandma was thankful when permanent-press clothing became available, because it drastically reduced the time needed to deal with laundry. She no longer had to sprinkle the clothing and put it in plastic bags to minimize the wrinkling before she got around to the ironing. Even so, Grandma's old sprinkle-bottle was still somewhere in the house. When all of the clothes were off the clotheslines, Grandma, with Mitzi accompanying her, took the laundry back up to the house.

By this time, it was often getting dark, and the dew was starting to appear. While Mom and Dad finished up in the garden, the grandchildren were content to go in the house and spend the rest of the evening with Grandma. Mitzi would come into the house with them, too, but Grandma didn't want her walking through the house with her little wet feet. Before Mitzi was allowed beyond the porch, Grandma bent down and used an old towel to wipe Mitzi's feet. One at a time, Mitzi patiently lifted each foot, so Grandma could dry it off. Then she was free to follow the grandchildren and ran off to the kitchen.

Grandma started a pot of coffee, because she insisted everyone have refreshments before they went home. The grandchildren played with Mitzi or some toys, or looked at some pictures or cards that were always in the living room. Or, they sat down and played the piano, maybe practicing some of the songs they were working on for piano lessons. Grandma sometimes came into the living room and told them that she liked every song they played.

Before long, Mom and Dad came into the house. They visited with Grandpa and Grandma as lunch was prepared. Then the children were summoned to the kitchen to eat. Grandma had their favorite orange or green Kool-Aid and her homemade doughnuts. After they finished lunch, it was time to go home. The grandchildren were tired. They wouldn't argue about going to bed on those nights, because chasing chickens and burning garbage was hard work. But even as they said good-bye to Grandpa and Grandma, the grandchildren were eager to come back again and help with the chores. There was something about the smell of smoke and sound of chickens against the backdrop of a country sunset that the grandchildren could never get enough of.

Chapter Fourteen
Grandpa's Place

Everyone has a favorite place. It might be a room or a chair, or maybe even a place outside. Frequently, with the passage of time, the memory of loved ones becomes more distinct when you revisit their favorite place. Grandpa's favorite place was at the dining room table. He would sit in a chair near the window writing letters, paying bills, and preparing his sermons. His writing tablet and his Bible were placed next to any bills that needed paying. There were always pens nearby, and Grandpa's little brass stamp-holder. Grandpa never bought books of stamps. He only bought stamps in a roll. He would write out a check and put it in a special envelope and leave it in the mailbox for the mailman. Then, when the mailman came to deliver mail, he found the envelope, took out the check, and left the stamps that Grandpa had paid for. When Grandpa brought the mail up to the house, he took the stamps out of the envelope and placed them in the little brass stamp-holder. The grandchildren were fascinated by the way Grandpa bought and stored stamps, and they loved helping him stamp envelopes.

Grandpa enjoyed writing letters and spent many happy hours in his chair next to the dining room window writing to missionaries, people in the church, or distant family members. People often told Grandpa how much they liked getting and reading his letters. When they wrote back, Grandpa always insisted on answering promptly. It was very important to Grandpa that he stay current with his letter-writing.

Grandpa also prepared his sermons while sitting at the dining room table. Next to his open Bible were scripture references written down on the backs of envelopes. It was not unusual to see a reference to Psalms on the back of the telephone bill or a notation from John on the back of the fuel bill.

Although you could find Grandpa sitting at the dining room table at any time of the day or evening, he preferred working on things early in the morning, after breakfast. The grandchildren often came into the house on a summer morning and found Grandma listening to the radio while she washed dishes in the kitchen. Then they found Grandpa in his customary place at the dining room table. He seemed to enjoy the cool morning breeze as it drifted through the dining room windows as much as he enjoyed hearing the sounds of the country: cattle in the steer yard, or tractors in the distance. This was home. Everything important in Grandpa's life—God, family, and the farm—came together here at the dining room table.

Chapter Fifteen
Bean-Walking

As the years passed, the grandchildren became old enough to help with other work on the farm. Often, the first time they were ever paid for working was when they helped with fieldwork. Bean-walking was a rite of passage for children who lived on a farm or in a rural community. Bean-walking was just that—walking up and down the rows of soybeans, pulling and hoeing weeds. Although tractors and other farm equipment could be taken into the cornfields to conquer the weeds, soybeans were shorter and bushier, which made it harder to navigate the farm equipment without damaging the soybean plants. Bean-walking was usually done in July, after the Fourth of July holiday. Every year, farmers talked about the "corn being knee-high by the Fourth." If it was, it meant that so far, it had been a very good growing season, and it would soon be time to start walking the beans.

Grandpa and Uncle Thomas always had some soybean fields, as well as some cornfields and alfalfa fields. Each year, they rotated crops planted in each field to make sure that the soil remained rich and conducive to farming.

The oldest grandchildren started walking beans when they were about twelve years old. As soon as they did, the younger grandchildren also wanted to help. It wasn't fair being left behind at the house with Grandma. They wanted to go out in the fields, too, and get paid. But some of the younger grandchildren were small for their age, and they had to wait not just until they were old enough, but big enough to work in the fields.

Because Grandpa and Uncle Thomas were family, working for them was different than working for other farmers in the area. If it was raining,

Grandpa would call early in the morning and tell the grandchildren they wouldn't work that day. Many other area farmers had their crews work in spite of the rain, canceling the work only if there was lightning. It was standard to work only in the morning, when it was coolest. Since Grandpa and Uncle Thomas had other chores to do each morning, they often thought that seven-thirty or eight o'clock was early enough to begin bean-walking. Other area farmers liked to start at six-thirty, or even six a.m.

Sometimes, the grandchildren would bring along some of their friends from school or the neighborhood. Mom might drive them all out to the farm; or Grandpa might come into town to get them. They went to the farmhouse first. Grandma filled large thermoses of water that they would take with them out to the field. Then they all piled into the back of the pick-up, and Grandpa and Uncle Thomas drove to the field. Although Grandpa and Uncle Thomas were always nice to everyone, they quickly identified the exceptional workers from those that were only good workers, and every year, they asked the grandchildren if the exceptional workers were able to come back.

Grandpa and Uncle Thomas's soybean rows were always less than a mile long. Some other farmers had mile-long rows, which meant you had to walk two miles to get back to the truck to get a drink of water. Grandpa and Uncle Thomas also planted their soybeans in nice, straight rows. A few farmers planted what Dad called "drilled beans," which meant the beans weren't in rows. They were thick, like grass, and very difficult to walk through, and even more difficult to weed, because it was hard to see the weeds among all the bean plants. Although those farmers may have thought that with more bean plants, they would get more beans and make more money, Dad said the beans didn't grow as well or yield as much when they were planted so close together.

The most common weeds in the soybeans were milkweed, mustard, cockleburs, and occasionally, thistles. The bean-walkers wore gloves, and they would usually pull everything except thistles. They hoed the thistles. Milkweeds could be very difficult to pull if they were tall. They had one main root that always seemed to grow as deep as the plant was tall. It was not unusual to fight with a milkweed and end up sitting on the ground when it finally yielded. If the milkweed broke off, the bean-walkers would see the white, milky liquid that the weed was named for. The liquid was very sticky, so the bean-walkers tried to avoid getting it on themselves.

Mustard plants often had pretty yellow flowers on them, which meant they also had bumblebees that the bean walkers had to beware of. The mustard plants could get very bushy, but their roots did not go very deep, so they were easy to pull out. Seeing the large mustard plants reminded the grandchildren of the parable of the mustard seed in the Bible: "such a small seed grew into a plant so large it could actually house birds in its branches." In some cases, that wasn't difficult to imagine.

Cockleburs could be the biggest challenge. They grew very fast, and their root network spread out as much as their leaves did above the ground. Grandpa said you had to be very careful with cockleburs. They did more damage to the beans than any other weed because of how they could choke them out. Grandpa also said you had to make sure that the cockleburs were pulled completely out of the ground and laid in the row to dry out in the sun. If they weren't pulled all the way out, the tiny bit of root still in the ground would be enough to revive the plant so that it would continue growing.

When it was close to noon, the bean-walkers returned to the truck and drove back to the farmhouse. Because some of the bean-walkers were her grandchildren, Grandma always insisted on making a big country dinner for everyone. The grandchildren's friends thought this was amazing. It was very unusual to go to work for someone who also fed you dinner with chicken or roast beef, boiled potatoes, vegetables, bread, Kool-Aid, doughnuts, and cookies. The bean-walkers always offered to help with the dishes, but Grandma always declined their assistance, probably because they were so dirty from the fields and she didn't want them handling her dishtowels.

After dinner, the bean-walkers collected their hoes, gloves, and water jugs for the ride back to town. Usually, it was Grandpa that drove them, until one day, when he ran a stop sign on one of the country roads. Thankfully, there were no other cars. In fact, the grandchildren couldn't ever remember seeing any cars on that road, but their friends were pretty shaken-up. That night, Mom insisted that Dad tell Uncle Thomas that from that point on, he had to be the one to drive the bean-walkers out to the field and back into town.

Bean-walking continued for several days. The whole bean-walking season usually lasted only two or three weeks, depending on the weather. On the last day of bean-walking, Grandpa sat down and wrote out checks to all the bean-walkers. He always thanked them for their help and invited them to come back again the following year. When all the checks had been distributed, the bean-walkers thanked Grandpa and Uncle Thomas for the work and Grandma for the wonderful meals. Then they piled into the car or the pick-up and talked about how they would spend their money, as Uncle Thomas drove them back to town.

Eventually, the grandchildren moved onto other jobs. There were part-time jobs during high school and college, and later, full-time jobs as the grandchildren established businesses and careers. But no job would ever be as important and no paycheck would ever be as meaningful as that first paycheck the grandchildren received for walking beans on Grandpa and Grandma's farm.

Chapter Sixteen
Grandpa's Church

Grandpa was the pastor for several churches in the small Lutheran synod he served, but he also had his own church. Worship services were infrequent, because there were very few remaining members by the time Grandpa became pastor. He was also gone many Sundays because of his responsibilities for other congregations. But, when he was home, those services were held in the same small white church that he had attended as a boy.

The country church dated back to the pioneer days. It was on a gravel road and stood on a small hill, which made its steeple visible for several miles. The church had no indoor plumbing and few other modern conveniences. As was the custom years ago, the worship was kept simple. There were no stained-glass windows and no organ; only an old upright piano. One-hundred-year-old pictures of the first founders and pastors still hung in the church narthex. A small lean-to was connected to the church, which provided access to the basement and kitchen.

When the grandchildren were very small, gatherings were still held at the old church. The family reunion was an annual event each summer. Nearly one hundred people would come from all over the country to gather at the little country church. Grandpa preached, Grandma played the piano, and everyone sang out of the little black hymnals. The grandchildren had never seen hymnals like this anywhere else. They were small black books, about three-by-four-by-two inches and contained only words, no musical notations. Dinner was, for the most part, potluck, but Grandma and several of the other women also cooked in the church kitchen. As was her custom, Grandma always made sure there were boiled potatoes for every meal.

Everyone ate dinner downstairs. The cool basement was filled with the wonderful aromas of food and good Norwegian egg coffee. Colorful summer dresses and lively conversation brightened up the gray concrete floor and walls. Children's laughter bounced off the concrete, adding to the noise level.

After dinner, the women washed the dishes. The men congregated outside to visit until the women were finished. As the adults reconvened in the basement and had their annual meeting, the children went outside. They played in the grass around the church, or they ran up and down the church steps. The only place they were not allowed to play was the church sanctuary. That was off-limits, because it was sacred.

Because it was the tallest thing on the prairie, the church steeple was frequently struck by lightning, but with no lasting damage. Even so, everyone attending the reunion got a little nervous if a summer storm developed while they were in church.

Gradually, the number of people attending the annual reunion declined, until one year, the reunion wasn't held. The annual summer gatherings had come to an end. The little country church now stood vacant one more week every year.

A couple of years after the final reunion, a tornado swept across the countryside and struck Grandpa's church. The entire building was picked up and set askew across the foundation. Facing significant repair expenses on a church seldom used, Grandpa was at a loss on how to proceed. While he contemplated, a group of local people asked for permission to move the church into town. Because it was historically significant, they wanted it available to the general population. They proposed making it a key exhibit at the county fairgrounds. Reluctantly, Grandpa agreed, knowing this was probably the best way to save the church he loved so much.

Grandpa still wanted a church building and found a small church in town that suited his needs. Its exterior resembled the country church, but everything else was different. The new church, thankfully, had indoor plumbing. The kitchen was more modern and better-equipped. The sanctuary was not as spartan as the country church and even had a small electronic organ, in addition to the piano.

The biggest difference was that the church in town would never experience the joy and laughter of a summer gathering. It would never host a family reunion. The grandchildren would always remember those times. Because of that, Grandpa's church would always be the little white clapboard church in the country. That little country church was a landmark for them, just as it had been a landmark for people one hundred years earlier, as they searched for its steeple across the endless prairie.

Chapter Seventeen
Grandpa's Funeral

The years passed, and one-by-one, the grandchildren began to ease into adulthood as they entered college and then the workforce. But as significant as those changes were, other things would impact them more. Some of those things would be of such a magnitude that life as they had known it would never be the same again.

It was a few days before Thanksgiving 1982 and, for Marlena, another first. It was the first time she was coming home from college for a holiday. She had caught a ride home with another student, a former high-school classmate. All of her excitement and happiness faded away as she walked into her parents' house. She wasn't even through the doorway before her sister gave her the news: "Grandpa died."

Grandpa had been "failing," as the adults liked to say, for the last few years. He'd had surgery and never fully recovered. He was weak and frail and easily confused. She remembered the last time she had seen him. He was in the hospital. Lying in the bed, her once strong grandfather looked old and small. She would be going away to college soon and wasn't sure when she would see Grandpa again. She felt she needed to tell him things she may not otherwise have a chance to say. As a stoic Scandinavian family, they weren't prone to outward, or even verbal, signs of affection. It just wasn't customary.

But there, in the hospital, she looked down at her grandfather, not sure that he would even hear or understand her, and she decided to break that Scandinavian silence. She leaned over Grandpa and told him she loved him and kissed him on the forehead. Grandpa reached out and took her hand and gripped it so firmly she thought her bones would break. Although feeble and consumed by illness, that one handshake contained all the remains of his former strength. The hand that held hers was one made strong by years of physical labor as he had coaxed the land to produce its bounty. The strength in that hand was that of a man decades younger; it was that of a robust man in his prime, not that of one approaching the end of his life.

Grandpa held her hand and would not let it go. It was then that the tears started to come. She looked down at her Grandpa as he held her hand, and she started to cry. Grandpa couldn't speak, and his eyes were closed, but the tears slipped through and started to roll down his cheeks. She knew she had to leave, but it was hard getting Grandpa to let go of her hand. Finally, she extricated herself from his grasp. Then she went out in the hallway and sobbed. No one quite knew what to do in the face of such an emotional display. Mom came after her a few minutes later to see if she was OK. She knew she had to be and dried her tears and said she would wait for them there. She couldn't go back to Grandpa's room.

Shortly after that, Grandpa went into a nursing home. Now, a few months later, he was gone. The next few days were a blur. The visitation was held at the funeral home the evening before the funeral. As expected, there was standing-room-only for the service. Somehow, she and her sister remained composed enough to sing. First, just the two of them sang an Amy Grant song, "El Shaddai,"—God Almighty. Then they sang "How Great Thou Art" with Uncle Thomas. They were all sure that Grandpa was there among them, listening.

The funeral was at Grandpa's church. It wasn't the old church in the country that they were familiar with. It was the small white church in town that Grandpa had gotten after the tornado struck the country church. There had never been any large gatherings or family reunions held at this church, not until today, when they gathered here to say good-bye to Grandpa.

Several pastors who had known Grandpa got up to speak and pay their respects. Uncle Thomas sang, and others prayed. Following the service, a luncheon was held in the church basement. It was the first time anyone could remember that Grandma wasn't downstairs making boiled potatoes. Grandma was doing surprisingly well. There were no tears, no outward signs of grief. She was a strong woman, and this was just another part of life that you got through. She visited with people, accepted their condolences, and thanked them for coming. Toward the end of the afternoon, one of her grandchildren told her that Grandpa would have approved. He always did enjoy a three-ring circus, and in his honor, they had had one!

As they were collecting their things to leave the church, everyone agreed that the family members should stop at Grandpa and Grandma's house before they went home. It was only a short drive from the church in town out to the farm. They had all been to the house other times when Grandpa wasn't home, but walking into the house this time was different. This time, Grandpa wasn't just out of town. This time, Grandpa wasn't coming back. It was hard to believe that, though. His ties still hung in the bedroom. His stamps and writing tablet were on the dining-room table, and letters were waiting to be answered.

The grandchildren wandered through the house, each lost in his or her own thoughts. No one really felt like visiting. They each wanted to remember Grandpa in their own way and, in his house, find their personal ways to say good-bye.

Marlena walked into the living room and went to sit in the chair where Grandpa always sat. His Bible was on the table next to the chair. Picking it up, she started to leaf through the pages, looking for comfort. There were notes in Grandpa's handwriting, pieces of paper with scripture references or sermon notations. Then she found an envelope in the New Testament. Although she didn't recognize the name on the back of the envelope, Grandpa had outlined a funeral service for someone. She turned to the verse in Second Timothy that Grandpa had referenced: "I have fought the good fight, I have finished the race, I have kept the faith." She smiled.

"Yes, Grandpa," she whispered, "you did fight the good fight. You did keep the faith. We will all miss you so much; but now, at last, you, too, have finished your race."

Chapter Eighteen
Visiting Grandma

Things were different after Grandpa died. The house was quieter with just Grandma and Uncle Thomas living there. Eventually, Grandma packed up Grandpa's clothes, and with each passing visit, there were fewer of Grandpa's things lying on the dining room table. After more than four decades of marriage, many people wondered how Grandma would carry on without Grandpa. As it turned out, the concern was misplaced. Grandma was still healthy and she decided she still had quite a bit of living to do and work to accomplish. Without a doubt, she missed Grandpa, but she never said a word about it to anyone. Certainly, she grieved for him, but no one ever saw her shed a tear. Any attempts at tiptoeing around Grandma's feelings would almost guarantee a tongue-lashing you wouldn't soon forget. Yes, Grandpa was gone, but there was still laundry to do, cows to milk, a garden to care for, and bills to pay. So everyone needed to get over their mourning and get up and get to work. Laziness was for the devil, and there was no time for laziness and self-pity when there was work to do. Grandma led by example, and this was the example she set.

Grandma settled into her new routine fairly quickly. Uncle Thomas took over Grandpa's few remaining church duties. Several times a year, it would be Grandma and Uncle Thomas who visited the small congregations, rather than Grandpa and Grandma. Although Grandpa had always paid the bills, Grandma assumed that responsibility like she had been doing it all of her life.

Grandma always enjoyed visitors. A day seldom went by that one of the neighbors or a family member or friend didn't stop by to visit with her. They could always count on a fresh cup of black coffee (and sugar lumps, if they were so inclined), homemade doughnuts, and some lively conversation, especially if it was an election year. With President Reagan's picture posted prominently on the bulletin board in the kitchen, Grandma made no secret of her political affiliations.

As the grandchildren passed from childhood to adulthood, the constant of going back to Grandma's house brought comfort and a sense of security and timelessness. The visits became less frequent because they had to be scheduled around college breaks or vacations from work, but the grandchildren looked forward to and enjoyed them as much as Grandma did. In fact, the older they got, the more they cherished these visits and talks with Grandma. They all shared special memories from childhood, but now Grandma also respected them as adults. She proudly told people what kind of work each of her grandchildren did. In Grandma's mind, a strong work ethic was akin to piety, and her grandchildren had not let her down in her expectations of them.

For the grandchildren, Grandma remained an anchor as they continued to explore this new, and sometimes frightening, adult world. Although many other things in their lives were changing, they could still go back to the house in the country, play the old piano, walk under the trees, and sit at the same kitchen table. Driving up to the house at Christmastime, they still saw the same electric candles lighting the dining-room windows. Grandma did very minimal Christmas decorating, but for years, she had placed the red plastic wreaths in the dining room windows. The wreaths had candles in the middle of them, and when they were plugged in, the electric bulbs would make the candles glow.

As they walked into the house those cold December evenings, they smelled the wood smoke from the old cookstove and felt its warmth as they entered the kitchen. Each year, like every year before, there would be baskets of Christmas cards and pictures to look through. As usual, Grandma insisted on serving lunch before anyone left for home. She still had hot chocolate for the grandchildren, though by this time, some of the grandchildren joined her for a cup of coffee instead. After lunch, Grandma walked them to the door, like she always had, said good-bye, and waited on the porch as they started their cars. Then, as the grandchildren started driving down the long driveway, they looked back to see the dining-room windows grow dark as Grandma turned off the candle lights on the old red Christmas wreaths. Another day had come to a close, and Grandma said a silent prayer of thanks as her grandchildren made their way home under the cold, dark Minnesota sky.

Chapter Nineteen
Making Lefse with Grandma

Smell is a powerful memory trigger, but food can also be a profound memory trigger, because so many family traditions revolve around food. Eating a particular type of meal can release all kinds of memories of people and past events, especially if that meal contains a favorite food. One of the grandchildren's favorites was *lefse*, a Scandinavian potato bread usually eaten with butter and sugar. It was generally made and eaten during the holiday season. The grandchildren always looked forward to Thanksgiving, because Grandma made sure there was plenty of lefse available between then and the New Year's holiday.

Sometimes, the grandchildren would not be able to get home for the holidays. Realizing how important some of those holiday traditions were to her grandchildren, Grandma insisted that they not miss out on them. She would wrap packages of lefse in zippered food bags, pack the bags into padded envelopes, and mail them to the grandchildren. Since they still lived in the frigid upper Midwest, it was never a problem keeping the special treat preserved during shipment.

As she got older, Grandma became frailer. It was harder for her to keep up with things, and making lefse became more difficult. During those later years, under Grandma's tutelage, Uncle Thomas learned how to make the family staple. Also at Grandma's direction, Uncle Thomas would pack up and mail the important packages to those grandchildren who may not get home for the holidays. The lefse-making skills had been safely passed onto another generation, since Uncle Thomas, Aunt Cheryl, and Aunt Rose now all knew how to make it. But none of the grandchildren knew anything about this culinary tradition. One year, two of the granddaughters decided to change that.

That year, Grace was still in college and home for Christmas break. Marlena was also home from the Chicago area. For all of them, visiting Grandma was a part of each visit home, and the grandchildren would always let Grandma know when they were coming. In early December, they said they wanted to see how lefse was made and asked if they could help Uncle Thomas make it when they came to visit. Grandma thought this was a fine idea, and they all looked forward to the upcoming visit.

Grace and Marlena arrived at the farm mid-morning on the designated day. Marlena was hoping to participate in every part of the lefse-making, so she was a little disappointed to see that Uncle Thomas had already prepared the dough. She told Grandma she had been expecting to help with that part also, but Grandma told her they would not have been able to make it if they hadn't prepared the dough ahead of time. She explained that the dough had to be thoroughly chilled before the lefse could be made. She said they would be helping with the part that was the hardest, which was the most important part for them to learn. She described to them how everything had been done up to that point. The potatoes were peeled and boiled. Then they were put through a ricer, making very finely-mashed potatoes. The right amounts of butter and flour were added to the mashed potatoes, and the dough was kneaded until it was well mixed. After the dough was thoroughly mixed, it was separated into four balls and placed in the refrigerator. Now it was time for Marlena and Grace to help with the next steps.

Lefse was made on a special griddle called a lefse iron, which Uncle Thomas had warmed up before the granddaughters arrived. A lefse board was also used. This was a large, round, clay-like disc that was used when rolling out the dough. Some boards had markings on them to help the cook determine what size the pieces should be, but if there were ever markings on Grandma's board, they had worn off years ago. The lefse board was covered with a white cotton cover. A special rolling pin was also used, which was covered with what looked like a white sock. The cotton-covering kept the dough from sticking to the rolling pin. The kitchen table was cleared except for the required implements, and Uncle Thomas was already working with one of the dough balls.

Grandma was sitting in her wheelchair next to the table, watching and advising. The granddaughters were eager to jump in and help, but Grandma suggested that they watch Uncle Thomas first. There was a real art to making lefse, and it was important to pick up all the little details. The granddaughters sat at the table and watched Uncle Thomas work, as Grandma explained what he was doing.

"First, you have to flour the lefse board and spread it out real good. Then put flour on the rolling pin and flour on your hands. Take one of the lefse balls, put it on the lefse board, sprinkle flour on it, and spread it out with your hands. Then take the rolling pin and start rolling it out, being careful to roll in only one direction. If the dough starts to stick, use more flour on the dough and the rolling pin. When the dough is about as thick as a sheet of parchment paper and about twelve to eighteen inches in diameter, it's ready to place on the lefse iron. The only way to move it from the lefse board to the lefse iron is with the lefse stick."

A lefse stick is approximately two-feet long and an inch-and-a-half wide. One end is rounded like a tongue depressor. The other end is the handle and the wood is a little thicker. Usually, the handles are painted in a pretty red and blue Scandinavian flower design.

"Now, the lefse stick needs to be placed on the lefse, about one inch away from an edge. The one-inch edge needs to be flipped over the stick. You then roll the stick away from that edge to roll the lefse sheet onto the stick. Carry it to the lefse iron. Lay the loose edge of the lefse on the edge of the lefse iron and unroll it, spreading it across the iron. It will cook quickly."

"How do you know when it's done?" Grace asked.

"When it starts to bubble or form light-brown spots, it needs to be turned," Grandma replied. "Place the stick under the middle of the lefse sheet, and pick it up so you can flip it like a pancake. When it bubbles and develops brown spots again, it is done."

"Then what do we do with it?" wondered Marlena.

"Take your stick and place it under the middle of the lefse sheet to pick it up," Grandma answered. "Remove it from the lefse iron, and place it on clean cotton dishtowels to cool."

After watching Uncle Thomas for a few minutes, the granddaughters were ready to try. Before long, they developed a rhythm. Marlena would roll and put the dough on the lefse iron; Grace would turn it and take it off. Thankfully, Grandma had two lefse sticks: a plain one that she had used all of her life, and a newer decorated one someone had given her. Although they were nervous about making a mistake or not having something turn out right, every piece of lefse came off the iron perfectly. Grandma complimented them on the good job they were doing, and she sat in her wheelchair with a proud smile on her face. As the granddaughters relaxed, they began to visit with Grandma and listened as she told them stories about making lefse as a girl.

"In those days, they didn't have lefse irons; we had to make it on top of the cookstove."

Grandma, of course, had a cookstove, and the smells of wood smoke and flour combined to give the kitchen a wonderful aroma. Feeling confident, Marlena asked Grandma if she could try to make the next piece of lefse on top of the cookstove.

"Sure," Grandma said.

Marlena put flour on the old stove, carefully rolled up the lefse, walked across the kitchen to the stove, and unrolled it. Since Grace needed more lefse for the iron, Marlena returned to the table and rolled out more for her. She and Grace watched the lefse on the stove, but it took much longer to cook there than it did on the lefse iron.

"Grandma," Marlena asked, "did it take this long to make when you used to make it on the cookstove?"

"Oh, yes," Grandma said. "Those stoves don't get as hot as the lefse irons, and the heat isn't as even in a wood-burning stove. You have to keep the fire up."

At that suggestion, Marlena decided to check the stove to see if it needed wood. Sure enough, it did; so she added more. After that, the lefse cooked a little quicker. In the meantime, Grace had already completed one piece, and she needed another for the lefse iron. Finally, the lefse on the cookstove was ready to be turned. The second side seemed to cook faster than the first side, but by now, Grace was already working on her third piece with the lefse iron. At last, the lefse on the cookstove was done.

"Wow, that's a lot of work," Marlena said.

"Yes, I know it is," Grandma replied, "but that's how we had to do it in those days."

"I think we'll just do the rest of it on the lefse iron," Marlena said. It was fun to do it the way Grandma had long ago, but once had been enough for her.

When he saw they knew how to make the lefse, Uncle Thomas left them to go do chores. Grandma and her granddaughters continued working in the kitchen until they had cooked everything Uncle Thomas had mixed. Grandma insisted they stay for dinner, and have fresh lefse of course, so the granddaughters started cleaning up the kitchen. There was lefse everywhere, but still, they weren't done.

"Now," Grandma said, "you have to cut the sheets into four pieces."

Marlena, after locating the kitchen shears and zippered bags, began cutting. Finally, it looked like what they were accustomed to eating. Grace folded the lefse and put it in the zippered bags. Grandma had them put some bags in the freezer for later use, but she made sure there were several bags left for the granddaughters to take home and share with their dad.

At noon, Uncle Thomas came back in the house and helped them get a simple meal prepared. They made sure there was a large plate with plenty of warm lefse and lots of butter and sugar. Grandma raved about how tasty it was and what a good job the girls had done. Uncle Thomas, too, said the lefse was delicious. Even though the girls normally ate several pieces of lefse, this time they had a little more than usual. After all, this time it was fresh, and it had never tasted better to them.

After eating, the granddaughters helped Uncle Thomas with the dishes and thanked him for helping and mixing the dough the night before. Uncle Thomas went outside to do more chores, and the grandchildren spent the afternoon visiting with Grandma. Finally, they saw she was tired and said they should leave for home. Grandma reminded them to take their bags of lefse. She said their dad would like having fresh lefse for supper. The granddaughters said their good-byes and thanked Grandma for the wonderful day. It had been one of their favorite visits with Grandma, and that morning, the secrets of lefse-making had been successfully passed on to yet another generation.

Chapter Twenty
Grandma's Good-Bye

No one is quite sure how it happened, but somewhere over the years, Grandma's family role changed. She had gone from a beloved, if sometimes stern, grandmother to a cherished and respected matriarch. The transformation was gradual. As the grandchildren married and began families of their own, there were other family members introduced to the role of grandparents, and Grandma's status evolved. She still brought wisdom and laughter into her children's and grandchildren's lives, but she also assumed the very special title of great-grandmother. A great-grandmother to talk to and visit is something none of the children and grandchildren had ever experienced, and they were thrilled that they could share this remarkable woman with yet another generation. But, as the tides and seasons of life shifted to accommodate these changes, everyone knew that they would shift again when Grandma went through her final transformation.

The call came around six-thirty a.m. on December 19, 1997. It was Mom, and Marlena could tell she had been crying. Grandma had died earlier that morning. As customary in those situations, the next few days were hectic for everyone. Aunt Cheryl and Aunt Rose arrived at the farm later that day. Mom and Dad, Uncle Thomas, Aunt Cheryl and Uncle Nathan, and Aunt Rose made the necessary arrangements for Grandma. The grandchildren adjusted work schedules and made the necessary travel plans.

Due to her physical frailty, Grandma had been in a nursing home for about the last one-and-a-half years of her life. Because she had been so fiercely independent, everyone was concerned about her adaptation to such structured living. Yet again, she surprised everyone by adjusting beautifully and making a whole new set of friends. She became a favorite among the staff for her sense of humor and conversational skills. Grandma was only there because of her physical limitations. Mentally, she was as young as any of those who helped care for her. She enjoyed discussing politics and current events, and she had a staunch opinion on every subject. She particularly enjoyed sharing her faith with others. Grandma's faith had been her ballast throughout her life and she wanted others to know how they, too, could find strength to endure any test or trial they might face. She became a mentor to some young women working at the nursing home. They, in turn, considered her their "grandma."

That afternoon, Mom and Dad, Uncle Thomas, Aunt Cheryl, and Aunt Rose went to the nursing home and gathered up Grandma's things. The young man on duty during Grandma's last hours was there and told them some amazing things. Typically, he never worked nights, only days, but for some strange reason, he worked the night before. Even more unusual, he agreed to work on his day off. He said he never worked on his day off, but for some reason, he decided he would this time.

Grandma had been extremely restless that night, and he was in her room at least fifty times throughout the night. Finally, when he went to her at four-thirty a.m., he said he couldn't stay with her, but he took off his nametag and pinned it to her nightgown. The young man was Catholic, and on his nametag were two pins, one of an angel and one of a cross. He took Grandma's hand and touched it to his nametag and told her about the angel and cross that were on there. He said that even though he couldn't stay with her, he was leaving his nametag so that in a way, she would know a part of him was still with her. The young man asked Grandma if she wanted him to call Uncle Thomas. Grandma asked him what time it was. When he told her it was four thirty in the morning, Grandma responded, "No, don't call him. You don't be getting people out of bed at this hour of the night. You wait until morning to call."

To her family, it seemed especially fitting that Grandma's parting words were to give an order. Even then, she could still command the same respect she always had. As children, that directness had been something they almost feared. Later, as adults, it was that same candidness that they had come to rely on and to cherish.

The young man said he left the room, and Grandma finally rested peacefully. He next entered her room at five fifty-five a.m. and knew immediately something wasn't right. Sometime between four-thirty and then, Grandma had died. He said it was as if she knew it was time to go, and even though she was a woman of great faith, she was still a little frightened in her last hours. Although she had been a staunch Lutheran all of her life, it was a young Catholic man who brought her comfort as she prepared to make her final journey. When he left his nametag with the pictures of the cross and the angel, she knew then that she wasn't alone.

Grandma had not been the only one restless that night. Twenty-five miles away, Dad, too, had been unable to sleep. Mom said usually if that happened, Dad was fine around two a.m., but not the night of December 18. That night, she said Dad was up and down all night, tossing and turning or pacing the floor. When the phone rang at five after six, he was in the kitchen to answer it before the first ring even completed.

One hundred fifty miles north, Grandma's granddaughter Cynthia was having trouble sleeping, too. Even though she was a sleep-deprived young mother with a seven-month-old daughter, she woke up far earlier than usual on the morning of December 19. She immediately checked on the baby to see if she had awakened her, but Bethany was sleeping peacefully. Fully alert and unable to get back to sleep, Cynthia got up. Not quite sure what to do at such an early hour, she decided the stillness of the house at quarter to six in the morning was conducive to decorating the Christmas tree.

The funeral was held on Monday, December 22, 1997. It was six days before Grandma's ninety-fourth birthday. The country church was filled to capacity with Grandma's family, friends, and all the people whose lives she had touched in such a special way. There were many beautiful floral arrangements, but none as poignant as the four red roses from her four great-grandchildren. Two of the great-grandchildren had colored special pictures that they had planned to give their great-grandma on their next visit. Although Grandma never got a chance to see them, the drawings were gently tucked beside her in the casket and would remain with her always.

Many of the nursing home staff attended but needed to stand in the back of the church because the pews were full. Some of the young staff women clung to Aunt Cheryl and Aunt Rose, crying and saying they felt as if they'd lost their own Grandma. One particularly distraught young woman said Grandma had really helped her through some difficult things in her life. She didn't know how she could go on without Grandma there to give her advice, but she knew her well enough to know that Grandma would expect her to be strong and face whatever lay ahead. Grandma had never stopped being an example and teacher. She freely shared with all those around her the same values and lessons she had instilled in her own family.

It was only three days before Christmas. Four days earlier, everyone had been frantic with Christmas preparations: last-minute shopping, baking, mailing Christmas cards. Now, those things didn't seem to matter quite so much. Aunt Cheryl said that's what Grandma would have wanted. She always got perturbed with people who seemed to put more importance on the trappings of the season rather than the meaning. Aunt Cheryl said this was causing all of them to slow down and focus on what was important: the meaning of Christmas—Jesus' birth and life and resurrection, our hope for eternal life, the promise of seeing loved ones again, and the importance of family. Yes, Christmas would be more subdued this year than it had been in years past, but it was still special.

Marlena, who lived in the Chicago area and was an organist, had not been home for a Christmas Eve since 1987. When she told her church that she needed to return to Minnesota for her grandmother's funeral, they told her to take an extra few days and, under the circumstances, spend Christmas with her family. Marlena said she didn't like the fact that it was a funeral that brought her home, but after so many years, she appreciated the opportunity to be home for both Christmas Eve and Christmas Day. Mom said it was like this was Grandma's last Christmas present to her.

At the conclusion of the funeral service, the family left the country church and accompanied Grandma's body to the cemetery. The road to the cemetery took Grandma past the place she had called home one last time. She would be buried next to Grandpa in a country cemetery, where generations of Grandpa's family had been laid to rest. Following the interment, the family made their way back to the church for condolences. They spent several hours visiting with people who had attended Grandma's funeral. It seemed as if everyone had a touching story or anecdote about this amazing woman they had called mom, mother-in-law, grandma, and great-grandma for all these years.

At the end of the day, the family returned to the farmhouse. As they walked into Grandma's house, they saw her Christmas cactus in the porch.

"Look," Marlena said, "it's filled with flowers! Isn't it beautiful?"

"Oh, yes," replied Aunt Cheryl. "It's been filled with buds since I came down here, and every day, I've been waiting for them to open. They finally all opened up this morning—the day of Grandma's funeral."

Grandma always had the last word. Now, with her Christmas cactus in full bloom, it seemed again as if Grandma whispered to them. In those pink flowers, the family found comfort and reassurance that Grandma was fine, and everything would be OK. For, as much as they already missed her, the family knew that this Christmas would be significant for another reason. After patiently waiting for her for so many years, this Christmas, Grandpa would once again be spending it with Grandma. Grandma had made it home in time for Christmas.

Chapter Twenty-One
The Auction

A few years after Grandma's death, Uncle Thomas married. Grandpa and Grandma's house again had a woman's touch, but it was far different than Grandma's. Although the grandchildren occasionally visited Uncle Thomas and his wife, the only familiar things were the cookstove in the kitchen and Grandma's old upright piano in the living room. As Uncle Thomas and his wife's first anniversary approached, everything was about to change again.

At his wife's urging, Uncle Thomas decided to sell the acreage containing the house and the outbuildings and move away. They broke the news to the family at the Thanksgiving gathering. The idea that strangers would be living in Grandpa and Grandma's house and that no one could ever go back there again was extremely unsettling to the whole family. After this shocking announcement, relations between Uncle Thomas and his wife and the rest of the family deteriorated. There was much discussion among the family, and Uncle Thomas was implored to take more time before making such a monumental decision, but he could not be persuaded. They were selling the farm site.

After much soul-searching and a few sleepless nights, Marlena decided to buy it, knowing the house would only be a vacation home. Her job, her career, her life was in Chicago and had been for many years. But her roots and part of her heart remained on Grandpa and Grandma's farm. Fully realizing the responsibilities and concerns of owning a place so far away, she talked to Mom and Dad before contacting Uncle Thomas. Her retired parents were only too happy to act as caretakers in exchange for maintaining their thirty-year gardening spot and seeing the farm site stay in the family. One thing remained before the sale closing and the beginning of this new partnership: the auction.

The auction was held the first Saturday in February. It was a gray, overcast, and blustery day, much in keeping with the family members' moods. As the first auction of the season, a large crowd was expected.

Even though they were an hour early, Marlena and Grace were the last family members to arrive. The driveway was already blocked off to prevent excess traffic on the grounds. Marlena had no other choice but to park her car alongside the gravel road, several hundred yards from the driveway. After driving to Grandpa and Grandma's freely for so many years, Marlena and Grace now felt like unwelcome strangers as they approached the roadblock.

Slowly and forlornly, Marlena and Grace walked up the long driveway. Recently-washed farm equipment was neatly lined-up to their right. Marlena saw the tractor that Dad had helped Grandpa and Uncle Thomas purchase years ago, when he was still single. Now, even though there was no sign, the words "for sale" were clearly communicated.

Marlena looked toward the house. On the yard sat several pieces of Grandpa and Grandma's furniture. As she continued up the driveway, all kinds of memories flashed through Marlena's mind. The furniture now stood where they had shared the joy and laughter of summer picnics. The cars parked along the gravel road converged with the endless procession of vehicles arriving for Christmas celebrations and Grandpa and Grandma's fortieth anniversary. Glancing toward the machine shed, she saw the auctioneer's trailer and visualized butchering chickens in the same spot.

Aunt Cheryl was the first to see Marlena and Grace arrive. Her warm hug brought all of Marlena's emotions to the surface, and she began weeping. Aunt Cheryl didn't say anything; she simply held Marlena and let her sob. Neither one cared that they stood in the middle of the yard and a crowd of people stared at them curiously. Marlena struggled for composure, knowing that if she didn't, she'd miss the auction. If she kept crying, it would be hours before she stopped.

"It's just so sad," she told Aunt Cheryl. "I looked at Grandpa and Grandma's furniture sitting over there, and it's like it had just been tossed aside like so much trash."

"I know," Aunt Cheryl replied. "I know; it's a very upsetting day for all of us."

The yard swarmed with people, and the crowd was estimated at six or seven hundred. It was hard to get an accurate count, because people were moving around, and nearly every farmer was wearing gold coveralls with a hooded sweatshirt or cap. People had come from three states and traveled more than one hundred miles to attend this event.

The auction was soon underway. Beforehand, the family members had conferred about who was interested in which items, so as not to bid against each other. It hurt them to realize that the only way they would have an heirloom of Grandpa and Grandma's would be by buying it through a public auction. The grandsons had winning bids for Grandpa's guns and some of the antique clocks. Aunt Rose got Grandpa's old wooden rocker. Ann, Cousin Will's wife, bought the bassinet that had held two generations of babies. Marlena purchased Grandpa and Grandma's dining room set and matching buffet, intending to put it back in the house when the property sale was finalized. Not everyone purchased something. Some of the grandchildren and other family members went away with nothing.

The auction for the small tools and household items went quickly. Aunt Rose and her friend Ruby left shortly afterward, because Aunt Rose was too upset to stay any longer. The crowd moved across the driveway when the bidding began on the farm equipment. Marlena, Cynthia, Grace, Mom, Aunt Cheryl, and the cousins continued to stand in the yard, trying to make sense out of what had just happened. They were all drained after such an emotionally wrenching experience. Then the threatening gray clouds released their fury. The snow came down in huge, fluffy flakes. What started as a few flurries quickly became a heavy snowfall. Marlena stood, motionless, next to the dining room table and buffet.

"What am I going to do? The wood will be ruined!"

Cynthia, Cousin Meredith, Cousin Will and his wife Ann, and Cousin Keith and his wife Sally quickly ran to their vehicles and retrieved blankets, sheets, and tarps to cover the antiques. Unfortunately, those offered only minimal protection. Will and Keith moved the furniture into the machine shed, knowing it was only a temporary solution. After Marlena purchased the furniture, Uncle Thomas's wife made it clear that she did not want it back in the house. It would be protected from the weather in the machine shed, but where could they go with it after that? Will discussed the matter with Uncle Nathan, who agreed to load the furniture on his trailer and take it to Mom and Dad's house. After such a difficult day, Marlena was quite moved by the help and support that her cousins and uncle gave her.

Meanwhile, the auction was still going strong. It took much longer to sell the farm equipment than it did the household goods, and after the farm equipment was sold, there was still livestock to be auctioned off. Marlena, Cynthia, Grace, Mom and Dad realized there was no point in waiting for the auction to finish and left.

Even though it was only a few weeks until she closed on the farm-site purchase, Marlena's heart was heavy as she walked down the long driveway toward her car. The family unit had been shaken, maybe to its very core, and no one was sure they would recover. As she placed one foot in front of the other, Marlena kept thinking, "What will we do now? Just what will any of us do?"

Chapter Twenty-Two
Thanksgiving

After Grandma's death, it seemed harder to find reasons for the family to get together. Even weddings and funerals, those time-honored occasions for most families to gather, found some family members absent. The grandchildren were busy with their young families and their jobs, and many of them lived in different cities, if not different states. But, unexpectedly, the auction became a turning point for re-establishing some of those family ties. After coming so close to losing the place they all loved, there was a renewed sense of importance on family gatherings like those the grandchildren had loved when they were growing up.

Two months after the auction, Marlena finalized the purchase of the farm site. For the next seven months, Mom and Dad had spent the better part of their time cleaning, painting, and planting. Mom still had her garden there, as she had for thirty years. Dad, previously unsure of what he would do in retirement, found all kinds of things to keep him busy back at his childhood home. Grace was out during the summer to help paint. No, nobody lived there full-time, but people were around nearly every day of the week, and it again looked and felt like Grandpa and Grandma's home.

Marlena's maternal grandmother, Grannie, moved into a nursing home a few weeks after the closing on the farm site. Through luck, fate, or divine intervention, Grannie's things could be moved from her house to the farm. That served a dual purpose; Marlena's house was suddenly furnished, and Grannie's things were much more secure than they would have been in her old, empty house.

In September, Marlena and Mom declared progress satisfactory enough to host the extended family Thanksgiving dinner at the farm. Invitations were sent, pies baked, and the house cleaned. Now, they simply waited for the rest of the family to find their way back home. Most of them hadn't returned since that difficult day in February when many of Grandpa and Grandma's things had been sold at the auction. Although some healing occurred, it had come slowly. Many of them made the long drive with a sense of fear or trepidation because of what had transpired that last tumultuous day they had been there. But mixed with that was also a sense of anxiety and expectation, because they knew this time would be different; this time it was about healing.

Marlena took several vacation days to be home and help with the preparations. Mom did all of the grocery shopping earlier in the week. Thanksgiving morning, Mom arrived at the farm at ten after seven. The first thing she said when she walked into the house was, "You should see how pretty it looks with the sun coming up over the silos. When I turned by the schoolhouse, it was gorgeous—just like a painting, with the sky all pink and blue and red."

Marlena got up at quarter to six to start a fire in the wood-burning stove. Since then, she, too, had been watching that painting take form and readily agreed with Mom.

The two of them set to work with a vengeance, chopping celery and onions, cleaning the turkey, cooking the giblets, mixing the dressing, and stuffing the bird. Once the turkey was in the oven, they started the next phase of preparations: coring the squash, cutting the apples, cooking the raisins, and filling the squash. Then came the potatoes. There was a mountain of potatoes to peel and cut. Mom, who had a great deal of experience with these kinds of meals, definitely took the lead. Marlena, a self-professed stranger to the kitchen, was only too happy to take orders and follow directions. Finally, all the food that could be prepared ahead of time was ready. Marlena and Mom sat down for a much-needed break and cup of coffee before turning back to wash all of the dishes.

Dad arrived at the farm a short time later with several gallons of fresh water and a few other things that Mom had asked him to bring along. After another quick break, Mom and Marlena began table-setting preparations. They were expecting twenty-two people and needed every leaf in both the dining room and kitchen tables. Mom brought the pretty cross-stitched Thanksgiving tablecloth she had made. That was placed on the dining-room table. She had another of her tablecloths for the kitchen table.

Grannie was coming from the nursing home and spending Thanksgiving with them. They used her good china dishes in the dining room and filled in with some of the other dishes. Earlier that year, Marlena and Mom had each found different sets of stoneware dishes. By the time they finished setting the tables, nearly every place-setting from all three sets of dishes was used.

Mom left for the nursing home to get Grannie, and Marlena left for the kitchen to tackle more dishes. When Grannie arrived, she was very pleased to see her pans being used to cook the Thanksgiving dinner and her china adorning the dining room table.

Cousin Keith and his family arrived shortly after eleven. His two children, four-year-old Stephen and two-year-old Kelsey, walked in hesitantly. They didn't really know these people or this house and weren't quite sure what to make of things. But Marlena and Mom had brought some toys from Mom and Dad's house, and before long, the children were happily engaged in play. Cousin Will and his family arrived a short time later. Six-year-old Nancy brought a turkey centerpiece that she had proudly made out of construction paper. She and Marlena went into the dining room to set him up on the buffet so he could grandly oversee all of the Thanksgiving festivities. Then Nancy, her sister Cindy, and brother Todd went off to play with their two cousins.

Marlena insisted that Mom give tours to everyone. This allowed them to reacquaint themselves with the house while seeing all the work that had been done. Shortly after the women went upstairs, Todd came with his dad, asking, "Can I go upstairs?"

Will said, "I told him he had to ask Cousin Marlena if he could go upstairs."

"Well, of course he can go upstairs! He's welcome here and can do whatever he likes!"

Before long, the other children realized there was more of the house to explore. Soon, the sounds of children's feet running up and down the stairs and throughout the second floor rooms echoed throughout the house.

Uncle Nathan, Aunt Cheryl, Cousin Meredith and husband Dennis, Cousin Charles and friend Ed were the next to arrive, followed by Grace and her friend Joey. Soon, the house was filled with laughter, voices, and the wonderful smells of turkey, coffee, and wood smoke. The children had lost their shyness and were having a glorious time playing with the toys and researching every corner of the old house.

Aunt Cheryl brought her five grandchildren to the kitchen and showed them the wood-burning stove and explained how wood needed to be added to the stove to keep the fire going. Then she opened the door that was next to the refrigerator. Behind the door were stairs that went up to nowhere. Grandma had always used the stairs as a pantry, stacking her canned goods on the steps. Meredith said she always remembered opening that door and seeing a can of fish-balls on the stairs. Aunt Cheryl explained that when she was a little girl, the stairs were open and went all the way up to the second floor. She asked her grandchildren if they remembered seeing the bathroom upstairs.

"Yes," they all answered.

When she was a girl, Aunt Cheryl explained, "The bathroom wasn't there. It was open. That's where these stairs came out."

One of her granddaughters looked confused as she went back to look at the other stairs she had just been playing on.

"Oh, those stairs were there, too," said Aunt Cheryl. "There were two sets of stairs. When we were little, we would chase each other up one set of stairs and down the other set of stairs all day long, and your great-grandma would get so mad at us for making such a racket!"

Each of Aunt Cheryl's grandchildren then went to look at the stairs in the kitchen, trying to imagine what that would be like. It was too bad those kitchen stairs didn't go anywhere any more, because chasing each other all around the house with two sets of stairs certainly sounded like fun!

Soon, the food was ready. The women had gathered in the kitchen to visit, and it took all of their help to get everything dished-up and placed on both of the tables. As had been the tradition for decades, the children were seated in the kitchen, and the adults were seated in the dining room. The ironic thing was some of those children seated in the kitchen were now the parents of some of the other children seated in the kitchen. The Thanksgiving meal was truly a feast: turkey, dressing, mashed potatoes, gravy, salad, squash, corn, dinner rolls, and lefse. Aunt Cheryl was the designated runner from the dining room to the kitchen, dishing up more things from the stove and making sure the salads made it from one room to the other. Everyone ate until they truly couldn't eat anymore, but then it was time for pie, and of course there would be room for that. Todd and Stephen, however, decided they'd had enough to eat and asked to be excused.

"What did they say?" Marlena asked.

"Oh, they want to go 'sploring,'" replied Aunt Cheryl.

Mom started cutting the pies while Aunt Cheryl, Meredith, and Cousin Will's wife Ann took requests. There were apple, blueberry, and pumpkin pies to choose from, with or without whipped cream. Dad came into the kitchen to ask about coffee, and Marlena, who had completely forgotten about it, started taking orders for coffee or other beverages. Finally, the meal was over. The pie and coffee had been the perfect cap to a wonderful meal. Eventually, the adults, too, decided they needed to leave the table. Ann and Sally, Cousin Keith's wife, started scraping plates and ordered Mom to sit down, saying she'd worked hard enough that day.

Aunt Cheryl headed for the sink and started running dishwater while Meredith looked for dishtowels. Marlena, Ann, and Sally continued to wrap-up the leftovers and gather the dishes. Soon, the entire kitchen table was covered with stacks of dirty plates, drifts of dirty silverware, and dozens of used glasses. But no one would have traded a single dirty dish for all the time they'd had together.

The women became a regular assembly line: Aunt Cheryl washing, Meredith drying, Ann and Sally putting away clean dishes, Marlena looking for more dishtowels and generally trying to direct where things were supposed to go. Before long, the children came in from outside. Stephen and Todd had their hands full of sticks and stood in front of the wood-burning stove.

"Put it in the fire," their little voices chimed.

"Well, that's why they were so eager to be done eating," said Aunt Cheryl, "they wanted to go outside to get wood for the stove!"

"Yes, they have the same fascination for the stove that we did," said Marlena. "I'm so happy they're able to have that same experience."

An hour later, the dishes were finally done. Dennis and Ed were napping in the living room. Charles and all the children had gone outside, and the other adults gathered in the dining room. Aunt Cheryl and Meredith pulled out their needlework and started stitching as everyone visited.

Marlena spent the week prior to Thanksgiving sorting through things that were in the attic. During that time, she had brought several boxes downstairs. Now, with her aunt, cousins, and sister gathered there, she told them that they were welcome to go through everything that was on the back porch and take anything they liked. They had gotten very little from the auction, and she knew they would cherish something that had belonged to Grandpa and Grandma. One-by-one, her cousins made their way to the porch, looking through piles of boxes, books, and pictures. Marlena had found several volumes of the same hymnal that Grandma had given her twenty-eight years earlier. She made sure her cousins knew there were enough to go around so that each of them could have a copy. She asked Ann if their three children took piano lessons.

"Not yet," said Ann, "we're hoping they can start lessons next year, but, even though they don't play yet, I would like one of those hymnals for them."

Will and Keith took boxes of pictures back to the dining room. There were all kinds of pictures: the really old ones from the early twentieth century, as well as the confirmation and graduation pictures. All of these had been left behind when Uncle Thomas and his wife had moved. Again and again, they asked Marlena, "You're sure you don't mind if we take these?"

"No, not at all. These belong to everyone. You're all welcome to anything that's here."

As she made her way back to the porch for more things, Marlena glanced out the window. It was a glorious, warm, sunny day. The door to the milk room of the barn was open. She figured the children must be down there, possibly looking for cats, although the cats were too wild to let the children near them. When Marlena looked up again, there was Charles walking in front of the silos toward the old hog barn. Following behind him, single-file, were his three nieces and two nephews, the younger ones half running to keep up with their uncle's long strides. Marlena smiled as she remembered being that age. She recalled many years earlier how much she and her sisters and cousins had enjoyed exploring everything there was to see on the farm, just like these children were today.

Marlena went to the back hallway for something else that was on the stair landing. It was a small, old, handmade wooden trunk that Mom had found during the first few days of her cleaning. Marlena picked it up and brought it to her Aunt Cheryl.

"Here, this is for you," Marlena said.

Slowly, Aunt Cheryl opened the trunk. Inside were some of Grandma's scarves. Aunt Cheryl's voice caught as she picked them up and held them to her face. Deeper inside, under some papers, were the real treasures. Aunt Cheryl picked up the first book.

"They're Grandma's cookbooks, and you should have them. They belong to you."

"Are you sure?"

"Oh, yes, I'm sure. You should have them; they're yours."

"But what about this trunk? You want this back, right?"

"No, absolutely not. You should have all of this. It's all yours to keep."

"Thank you; thank you so much," Aunt Cheryl said with tears in her eyes, as she looked at Marlena.

They spent the afternoon reminiscing, telling the stories behind the pictures and sharing their happiest memories of being children in Grandpa and Grandma's house. The shadows grew longer, and the warm fall afternoon rapidly began to cool. The children came in, made sure there was still wood burning in the cookstove, and went off to run up and down the stairs or play the piano—the same piano that their great-grandmother had played when she was a girl.

Finally, someone mentioned something about getting ready to go. But, no! No one could leave yet! Lunch still had to be served! Mom, Marlena,

Aunt Cheryl, Meredith, Ann, and Sally went back into the kitchen for the second round of food service. Lunch was far easier to launch than the Thanksgiving meal, but with less adrenaline flowing, it still required a collective effort. It was the traditional lunch that Grandma would have served: cold turkey, dinner rolls, lefse (with butter and sugar, of course), pie, and fresh coffee. Even after lunch, people still lingered, unwilling to have such a happy day come to an end.

Finally, Keith and Will insisted the children come into the living room and pick up the toys they had played with. Marlena and Mom were in the kitchen making care packages of food and finding the dishes everyone had brought. It was dark enough that the porch light had to go on as people gathered up their coats and got ready to leave. It was then that Aunt Cheryl and Cousin Charles noticed Grandma's Christmas cactus in the porch. This, too, had been left. The plant was huge. It had become so large that it sat on a utility cart and had to be wheeled from room to room.

"They left the cactus!"

"Yes, and Mom's been taking great care of it," Marlena said.

"That was Grandma's, you know."

"Oh, yes, I know. She loved that plant; I'm glad it's still doing well. She had it for so many years."

"It was her mother's before that."

"Her mother's! I didn't know that!"

"Oh, yes. You know her mother died, and Grandma had to help raise her brothers and sister. Well, when she and Grandpa got married, she took her mother's cactus with her."

"But Grandma would have been ninety-nine years old this year! That means that plant must be between one hundred and one hundred fifty years old!"

"Yes, it is, and it's been here for most of those years. I'm glad they left it; it belongs here."

There were more thank-yous and more good-byes. Then, as Grandma and Grandpa had done so many times before, Mom, Dad, and Marlena stood on the porch and waved good-bye as the others got in their cars, made their way down the long driveway, and headed home.

Chapter Twenty-Three
The Open House

Thanksgiving had brought healing. In the words of the old Thanksgiving hymn, the family had gathered together and been blessed. By reinstating some of the old traditions, they had realized how meaningful they still were. No, it wasn't easy to get everyone together. Distance, work, school, extra-curricular activities, and other commitments definitely made it a challenge, but it was possible. It wouldn't just happen. It would certainly take planning, and maybe not everyone could be there, but the important thing was, you got together anyway. The only thing sadder than family members missing from the family gathering would be no family gathering at all. It was with that spirit that Mom and Marlena planned the next family get-together.

As she had for so many years, Marlena planned to be home for a few days after Christmas. Since Christmas was on a Wednesday, and most people were usually busy on the Sunday between Christmas and New Year's, Marlena and Mom decided they would have an open house on that Saturday, December twenty-eighth. There wouldn't be a large-scale meal this time, just an afternoon get-together with sandwiches, cider, coffee, hot chocolate, and dozens of Mom's fancy homemade Christmas cookies, fudge, and candy. They would invite the family to stop in for the afternoon, but this time, they also invited the neighbors. The neighbors, many of whom had known Grandpa and Grandma years before, had been so gracious and helpful that first year. They had seen how often Mom and Dad had been out there working, and Marlena wanted to give them an opportunity to come in and see all the work that had been done inside as well.

Saturday, December twenty-eighth dawned warm and bright. It was a rare Minnesota Christmas without snow. Mom and Dad decided to come out to the farm for the noon meal. Mom and Marlena had dozens of sandwiches to make, and the open house began at two o'clock, so it was easier for them to come early. Marlena had made a casserole, and the three of them sat down to eat at the old kitchen table, as they had so many years ago with Grandpa and Grandma.

Mom brought her pretty serving plates and large coffeepot for making the cider. As Marlena washed the dishes, Mom prepared the cider, and soon, the wonderful smell of cinnamon and mulling spices mixed with the scent of the wood smoke from the old wood-burning stove.

When the dishes were done, Marlena and Mom buttered the buns for the sandwiches and filled them with turkey or roast beef. With both of them working at the kitchen table, the four dozen sandwiches were quickly completed. Then it was time for the fun part: putting all the cookies on the serving plates. Since Mom had made all of the special cookies, Marlena decided it only made sense to let her provide the final touches by arranging them on the plates. Mom had also brought some of her homemade pickles. These were served in Grannie's pickle dishes. Unfortunately, Grannie wouldn't be joining them that afternoon, because she hadn't been feeling well the last few days.

Before long, the dining-room table was artfully displayed with a mind-boggling assortment of Christmas delicacies. After Thanksgiving, Mom and Marlena had set-up Grannie's Christmas tree in the living room and added several other decorative Christmas touches to the house. At two o'clock, they plugged in the Christmas lights, lit the candles on the dining room table, started the Christmas carols on the CD player, and waited.

Unfortunately, most of the cousins weren't expected. Sally called that morning to say the children were sick. Will and his family had other commitments, and Charles was working. But Aunt Rose had called Marlena the night before to see if she should bring anything and also ask if she and Ruby could bring their dog.

"Of course she can come," Marlena said, "I love animals!"

About quarter after two, they saw Aunt Rose's blue Cadillac coming down the gravel road. When they pulled in the driveway, Aunt Rose, Ruby, Uncle Nathan, Aunt Cheryl, Meredith, and a fluffy little Pomeranian dog all piled out of the car. Aunt Rose had not been back to the farm since the auction in February, and after a few minutes' hesitation, she went into the house. Even before she left the front porch, she remarked how nice the house looked. Mom served as tour guide, like she had at Thanksgiving, and showed Aunt Rose and Ruby the house. When Aunt Rose stepped into the dining room, she stopped, looked at the table filled with Christmas goodies, saw Grandpa and Grandma's buffet back against the wall as it had been years before, and remarked, "Mom would be proud."

This was the greatest compliment Mom could have received, and she replied, "Thank you. I so enjoyed doing all of this and trying to make it look like it used to."

The tour continued through the bedroom, living room, and second floor. Afterward, Aunt Rose seemed far more relaxed than she had been when she arrived. Later, she would tell Marlena that it seemed like home again, and that once more, she felt comfortable being there.

They gathered in the dining room and visited. Meredith and Aunt Cheryl, always prepared, pulled out their needlework and knitted and stitched away as they talked. The other guests arrived a short time later. Terrence and Claudia, a brother and sister who lived on a neighboring farm, had driven over for the afternoon. They had known Dad, Aunt Cheryl, and Aunt Rose when they were children. Claudia and Aunt Cheryl had a delightful time reminiscing and getting caught up on each other's lives.

Lyle, another neighbor, stopped by. He said the gathering, with coffee brewing, food on the table, and visitors present, reminded him of all those other times he'd been over when Grandma had a house full of people around Christmastime. Grace and her friend Joey came. Right behind them were two other neighbors who knew Joey. As usual, the men retreated to the sun-filled living room and talked about weather and crops, while most of the women congregated in the dining room, laughing, talking, and eating. With the fire in the wood-burning stove and the house full of people, it got quite warm. Aunt Cheryl took off her jacket and went to lay it on the bed in the bedroom.

She came back, sat next to Marlena, and whispered, "I just had to do that. We always went and laid our coats on Mom's bed when we were here."

"And I'm so glad you did," replied Marlena with a smile on her face. That was exactly what she wanted—people feeling comfortable and things being like they were before.

The afternoon passed quickly, and before long, people were gathering their things to leave. A wonderful time was had by all, and everyone expressed their thanks as they said good-bye. This was, after all, a special day, but Marlena did not realize how special until someone pointed it out.

Unknowingly, she had planned this very special Christmas open house on what would have been Grandma's ninety-ninth birthday. Once again, Grandma's house had been filled with people, laughter, and good food. Once again, there had been a celebration in the house on Grandma's birthday. That evening, as she stood in the dining room, Marlena looked at Grandpa and Grandma's wedding picture hanging on the wall, over-looking the dining room table.

"Happy birthday, Grandma," she said as she turned out the lights and blew out the Christmas candles. "Happy birthday."

Chapter Twenty-Four
Final Resting Place

No matter how many times you've done it before, saying good-bye to a beloved family member is never easy. Nothing really prepares you for those bittersweet partings. Each time brings new tears and new grief, and finally, new healing. So began another good-bye on a snowy winter day. It was one of those rare April Minnesota blizzards. Although they didn't happen often, this one came on with a vengeance. Mom, as she had been for so many weeks, was up at Cynthia's house. Cynthia and Winston's baby boy was born in December, a few weeks before Winston had to leave for an extended training program. With two young daughters and newborn son, everyone agreed that Cynthia needed help while Winston was away, and Mom had been only too happy to volunteer.

Now it was Mom's last week before Winston came home. She and Cynthia had heard on the news about a fierce winter storm back home. When Dad called early that morning, they suspected the storm was the reason. Unfortunately, it was something else. Rudy, the dog Mom and Dad had gotten for Grace thirteen years earlier, was sick. When he described what was going on, Mom told Dad, "Get Rudy to the vet."

The storm was vicious, and Dad had to blow snow from the driveway before he could move the car out. Finally, he put Rudy in the car and went to the vet's office. The prognosis was bad—terminal, actually. Rudy had developed blood clots and would need to be put to sleep. Dad, unwilling to let that happen without talking to Grace, said he understood, but he needed to talk to his daughter, since it was her dog. He tried to call her, but there was no answer. Loading Rudy back into the car, he decided to stop at Grace's apartment on the way home. He drove across town in a blinding snowstorm with a dying dog in the car, and he hoped he'd find his daughter at home. She wasn't. With little choice, Dad and Rudy went back home. It was only a few minutes after he carried her back into the house that Rudy died.

Mom got her second call at Cynthia's that morning. "Rudy's gone," Dad choked out between the tears. "I couldn't get hold of Grace."

Mom remembered Grace had once given her Joey's cell phone number. "Try that," Mom said. "See if she might be with him because the weather's so bad."

Grace, indeed, was with Joey when she found out that her childhood companion had died. There had been no opportunity for either Grace or Rudy to say good-bye. Although they had discussed the situation previously, Grace surprised her parents when she told Dad, "I want Rudy buried out at the farm, under the apple tree."

The previous summer was Rudy's first opportunity to spend time on the farm. She made friends with the cats and explored the woods. As she ran under the trees with her ears flying behind her, she behaved like a happy little puppy, not the senior dog she had become. In her twilight years, she had found the equivalent of a canine retreat. Like every other family member, Rudy relished the time she spent at the farm.

In the ensuing conversation with Dad, Grace outlined specific plans for her dog. No, Grace didn't want to see Rudy one last time. No, she didn't want Rudy's collar. Rudy had always worn her collar, and she should be buried with it. Because of the storm, Mom couldn't come home and say good-bye to Rudy, either. The messy business of death and burial was left to Dad to deal with—alone.

The storm raged on. Dad had no hope of getting Rudy out to the farm that day. Instead, he placed her body in the garage until the roads were passable. Mom told Dad where he could find an appropriate-sized cardboard box that could be used as Rudy's coffin. Into that box Dad placed their little friend, wrapped in her favorite rugs and blankets.

The next day was sunny and warm. The snow from the day before would melt quickly. Dad drove out to the farm with his shovel and Rudy. He and Mom had talked about where under the apple tree he should dig the grave. Slowly, shovelful by shovelful, Dad dug. When the hole was about two feet deep, he placed the cardboard coffin in Rudy's final resting place. Grace's wish had been granted; Rudy was buried under the apple tree on the farm.

Mom came home a few days later. The house was extremely empty without the sounds of little canine feet. Rudy had died on her thirteenth birthday. The family had always easily remembered Rudy's birthday, because she had shared it with another very special family member—Grandpa. He would have been ninety-nine years old the day Rudy turned thirteen. It was fitting that her burial place was on Grandpa's farm under the apple tree that he had lovingly planted and cared for. Although their lives had not intersected, each of them—the beloved little dog and the family patriarch—touched the other family members' lives in both ordinary and extraordinary ways. Now together, their memories were entwined on the family farm.

Later that week, Mom and Grace talked about somehow marking the place where Rudy was buried. They agreed to plant daisies on Rudy's grave, and, a little further from the apple tree, a dogwood bush.

Spring came quickly after that April storm. Once again, the earth brought forth new life, and everything was green and new and fresh. Before long, Dad was mowing lawn and tilling the garden soil. Mom was weeding flowers and planting vegetables. Always, there was the sense of Grandpa and Grandma's presence. Years ago, Aunt Rose had given Grandpa asparagus. Together, at Grandpa's insistence, he and Mom had planted it. Now, every spring, as it pushed through the soil, it was as though Grandpa, too, had stopped by to greet them. As the laundry blew on the clotheslines, it was hard to remember that Mom had put it there, not Grandma, pulling her little red laundry wagon behind her. Rudy was there with them, too, although she wasn't running around and barking. She rested under the apple tree, not too far from the garden, and in the shade of the old cottonwood tree. Rudy, too, had come home.

Yes, the old cottonwood tree with its white lightning stripe down its trunk still stood strong and tall, towering over every other tree on the farm. It, too, had awakened from its winter rest. Now, as the wind blew through its branches, it seemed to call to them: "From wherever you are, you're welcome here. However long your journey, here, in this place, you will find comfort and rest. Together, may you reminisce about happy times. May you also create new memories in the days and years ahead. In this place, you are special; for in this place, you are home."

978-0-595-43946-1
0-595-43946-2